Unlimited
Innovation
by NTT

The
Identity
of
IOWN

President,
CEO of NTT
Akira Shimada

Senior Executive Vice President,
CTO of NTT
Katsuhiko Kawazoe

Nikkei BP

Preface

Global electricity consumption is increasing at a rapid pace. Despite efforts to reduce that usage, recent advances in digitalization have led to a surge in the amount of data in need of processing, while the appearance of generative AI, which requires computing on a massive scale, has spurred yet more power usage. For example, training a major generative AI tool requires electricity equivalent to one hour of output from a nuclear power plant. As a society, we face serious questions on how we can reduce the power that digital technology consumes.

The price of humanity's rapid industrial development has been the heavy burden placed upon the Earth. Climate change in particular has begun exerting a serious impact around the world, making it imperative that we achieve carbon neutrality through such measures as lower power consumption and a greater share of renewables in our energy mix. And looking at the bigger picture, the greatest challenge we face is how to achieve global sustainability.

Meanwhile, the internet, which has transformed our lives through digitalization and otherwise, also poses major challenges.

The internet has brought us many benefits. Our society is now so dependent on this infrastructure that it would cease to function without it. One problem with the internet, however, is that it is premised upon best-effort delivery, which means no guarantees about the quality of a transmission. You cannot determine beforehand when the data you send will reach its recipient, nor when you will receive data sent to you. Furthermore, latency can vary according to network conditions. Therefore, it is quite impossible to use the internet, which operates on a best-effort basis in an unstable communications environment, for certain essential functions such as financial transactions where the exact timing of an order can make the difference between its success or failure.

There is a way to simultaneously solve both of these issues—the challenges posed by the internet and the need to conserve power to ensure global sustainability—and thereby create a smarter society: the IOWN Initiative, which is the topic of this book.

IOWN (Innovative Optical and Wireless Network) is a technology platform based on "light". At NTT, we have spent many years pioneering research on the use of optical fiber to achieve high-speed, high-capacity communications. Humanity has traditionally used electricity to transmit signals from networks to computers, but by replacing that electricity with light, we can dramatically reduce power consumption while achieving stable data transmissions with low latency, at high speed, and at a high capacity.

We announced the IOWN Initiative in May 2019, and in 2020 we established the IOWN Global Forum, a joint effort between NTT, Intel, and Sony (now the Sony Group). As of September 2024, more than 150 companies and organizations from across the globe have joined this group, where we are proactively working on projects ranging from developing technology and defining specifications to running Proof-of-Concept tests. And March 2023 saw the launch of APN IOWN 1.0, the first service to come out of the IOWN Initiative. This marked our long-awaited entry into the commercialization phase.

What exactly is this IOWN technology that is quickly spreading across the planet? This book will show you. As you can gather from the fact that the IOWN Global Forum is at the heart of promotional efforts, IOWN is something that NTT is building not on its own, but with all of you. In the future, we expect to see a steady stream of new businesses emerging from this initiative.

And when it comes to ensuring global sustainability, we must not be complacent, as we cannot expect somebody else to improve the situation for us. It is crucial that we take it upon ourselves to act. My hope is that through this book, you will come to understand and endorse the IOWN Initiative, and that you will join us in action to create a more sustainable planet through this initiative.

Akira Shimada
President, CEO of NTT

Table of Contents

2   Preface

13   Introduction: A Light of Hope for Global Sustainability

14   IOWN, Essential to a Sustainable Planet

Contributions to creating a sustainable society with exceptionally low power consumption

The coming explosion of data

The need for data-driven solutions to social issues

The problem of faster power consumption due to the growth of generative AI

Should we halt technological innovation when a problem comes up?

Light: the way to use less power

22   Roadmap of Advancements Toward 100x Better Power Efficiency

Latency is already down to 1/200th

IOWN 2.0 to connect boards with light at Expo 2025 Osaka, Kansai, Japan

27   Co-creation with Partners

Establishment of the IOWN Global Forum in the United States

Incredibly lower power consumption will contribute to planetary sustainability

33 Chapter 1 – Commercial IOWN in Action

34 Initial Impact of Spread

The first mention of IOWN at a U.S.-Japan summit

The long-awaited launch of commercial services

Unnoticeable ultra-low latency for music and sports

Creating the first international IOWN APN connection

40 Training Programs Kick Off

Training program to produce IOWN pros

42 Why IOWN Is a Game Changer

From the telephone to the internet, and now IOWN

The internet and a seismic shift in society

Signs of the internet's limitations

IOWN will bring time synchronization back to the network

Conversations between AI chatbots also need accurate time synchronization

The economic logic of the internet : a double-edged sword

It all started with a research paper published in 2019

50 Redefining Data Centers

The issue of where to build data centers

Proof-of-Concept test along 100km between Yokosuka and Mitaka

Enabling local energy production and consumption

The next step: computing

57 Chapter 2 – The Impact of Photonics-Electronics Convergence Devices

58 Expanding IOWN from Networks to Computing

Expanding photonics-electronics convergence technology to smaller devices and chips

61 Massive Data Center Efficiency Gains with IOWN 2.0

Connecting components with light to transcend the "box"

Next-generation disaggregated computing

Disaggregated computing Proof-of-Concept tests already conducted

66 Optical Semiconductor Chips Will Meet the Demands of the AI Era

The "three arrows" for boosting chip performance

The first arrow: miniaturization

The second arrow: high-density packaging

The third arrow: optical communication between chips

NTT's membrane technology supporting optical advancesments

75 Developing Photonics-Electronics Convergence Devices In-House and Automating an Art

Provide devices after establishing production and mounting processes

Building a global ecosystem with many corporate partners

79 Chapter 3 – Finding Partners for a Global Platform

80 The IOWN Global Forum, Founded with Intel and Sony

Expectations exceeded with over 150 members

Weekly meetings ahead of the forum's creation fostered unity

Documentation produced in online meetings until the first in-person conference in the fall of 2022

85 Dual Focus on Technology and Use Cases

Tech and user company participation creates a virtuous cycle

Embarking on Proof-of-Concept testing

89 Two Categories of Use Cases to Implement

AI communication

Cyber-physical systems

95 The IOWN Global Forum's Vision for the Future

Promptly starting up businesses is more persuasive

97 Key People Speak on the IOWN Global Forum

For a Sustainable Future
Rong-Shy Lin, President, Chunghwa Telecom

Looking Forward to Strong Leadership
Gilles Bourdon, Vice President of Wireline Networks & Infrastructure, Orange Innovation

103   Chapter 4 – The Future IOWN Will Bring About

104   IOWN & AI

A starting point to addressing AI-related problems

NTT's proprietary LLM: tsuzumi

AI needs diversity, too

AI constellations will reveal lines of reasoning

Efficient collaboration between multiple AIs

Four use cases for AI constellations

120   IOWN & Quantum Computers

Quantum computing, the ultimate goal of IOWN

122   IOWN in the Wider Society

Construction: remotely operated construction machinery to address labor shortages

Medicine: telehealth to correct regional disparities in care

Broadcasting: remote production to enhance live broadcasts

Data backup: distributing backups in real time

Esports: creating fair online competitions free from latency's impact

Smart cities: an information distribution platform for big data

Space communications: a new future for space exploration with light data relays and HAPS

135 Chapter 5 – Data Security and IOWN

136 Safeguarding the State's Data

The state is the data which defines it

139 Backups Aren't Enough

Data movement to protect important information

What is a safe place to store data?

Data holds the same importance for companies

IOWN can safeguard organization-defining data

145 Final Chapter – From the Logic of Quantity to the Logic of Values

146 From Quality to Quantity, from Quantity to Values

Japan lost out on the logic of quantity

Amassing quantity requires a global start

Lessons learned now applied to the IOWN Global Forum

Toward a logic of values fostering mutual respect

New social infrastructure requires a new philosophy

Aiming for a society with multiple layers of values

154 From the Digital to the Natural

156 What Is the Identity of IOWN?

158 Afterword

162 Reference List

164 Writing Contributors

[Introduction]

A Light of Hope
for Global Sustainability

IOWN, Essential to a Sustainable Planet

"Innovating a Sustainable Future for People and Planet."

This was the message in one of NTT's TV commercials. It is the basic concept behind our approach, "New value creation & Sustainability 2027: powered by IOWN," in the NTT Group's Medium-Term Management Strategy. It also clearly demonstrates the NTT Group's commitment to taking on the challenge of creating a sustainable planet and society.

Society now faces numerous problems in need of solutions in many areas, such as climate change, biodiversity, and health care. To address these issues and create a sustainable society, some say it is essential that we adopt a "data-

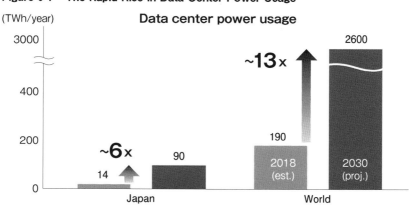

Figure 0-1 – The Rapid Rise in Data Center Power Usage

Source: Center for Low Carbon Society Strategy, Japan Science and Technology Agency

driven" approach, which entails the collection and analysis of large amounts of data to identify optimal solutions. However, the more data we have, the more power consumed by the data centers processing it (Figure 0-1). The fact is, this rapid increase in power consumption could be a major obstacle to creating a sustainable society.

The IOWN Initiative, the topic of this book, is the game changer that will solve this dilemma. As the inclusion of the phrase "Powered by IOWN" in the name of the NTT Group's Medium-Term Management Strategy shows, we are directing all our efforts toward promoting this initiative to create a sustainable society.

Contributions to creating a sustainable society with exceptionally low power consumption

IOWN is a new network and computing technology platform based on years of NTT Group R&D on optical technology. By using optical signals to replace the electrical signals used in communications and computation, we will enable functions that were previously impossible. Optical signals will also allow us to drive the rate of power consumption from processing data for communications or computing down to one-hundredth the amount we use now. The IOWN technology platform has an enormous range of potential applications, from long-distance international networks to the nanoscale wiring inside computers.

To dramatically lower this power usage, there are limits to what we can do through further improvements in semiconductor technology that is based on conventional electrical signals. We believe that the key to guiding society toward sustainability with low power consumption is to fundamentally shift networks and computing from electricity to light through IOWN.

The coming explosion of data

Let us take a more in-depth look at the situation society now faces.

Firstly, humanity has been generating a steadily increasing amount of data in recent years, and that rate is set to accelerate exponentially. For example, the quality of the videos we enjoy is getting better and better. Even with an ordinary smartphone, today we can easily shoot and watch high-definition 4K video. The trend toward higher resolution will expand to a much wider range of applications, including dashcams and the surveillance cameras installed around our cities. Ultra-high-definition video with 16K resolution contains approximately 750 times the data in current full HD video. Naturally, we can only handle 16K data effectively if we upgrade our networks and devices to handle 750 times more data.

Another factor contributing to greater data volume is the spread of virtual spaces in the metaverse. For example, estimates indicate that holding an online meeting in a three-dimensional setting in the metaverse, rather than with traditional two-dimensional images, requires about thirty times as much data. Another important task is the collection of real-world data, and this is expected to grow rapidly. The Internet of Things (IoT), by which objects are connected to the internet, seems set to spread at a faster pace, allowing us to obtain data from more and more of the things around us. According to predictions, the number of devices connected to the internet will increase to 125 billion by 2030, an increase of about fivefold from 2017. As a result,

Figure 0-2 – An Explosion of Data

Higher resolution in video	3D data	IoT advancements

Higher resolution in video
Full hi-vision
1.5 Gbps
→ 16K footage
1147 Gbps
~750x
* Theoretical values with uncompressed footage

3D data
2D data
→ Metaverse (VR)
~30x
Source: Cisco Annual Internet Report (2018-2023) If compressed UHD footage

IoT advancements
More connected devices
2017
27 bn
~5x → 2030
125 bn
Source: IHS Markit

Projected data growth Unit: bytes
1 exabyte (EB) = 1 quintillion (10^{18}). →1000EB = 1 zettabyte (ZB). →1000ZB = 1 yottabyte (YB)

1 YB

6.2 EB	988 EB	44 ZB	Up ~20x
2000	2010	2020	2028-36 (proj.)

Source: Ministry of Internal Affairs and Communications white paper (Nihon Keizai Shimbun, May 16, 2023)

global data traffic will grow by more than twenty times between 2028 and 2036 (Figure 0-2).

The need for data-driven solutions to social issues

As stated near the beginning of this chapter, to tackle the social issues our planet faces, it is critical that we adopt a data-driven approach that emphasizes the importance of this information at our disposal. Whether the issue is climate change, biodiversity conservation, or health care, it is essential that we obtain detailed data and utilize it in real time so that we can manage and improve the situation.

Take the fight against climate change, for example. By closely monitoring what changes are occurring in what areas, we can begin to understand the mechanisms at work and the scope of the impact. In terms of nature-positive efforts to restore biodiversity, the first step in devising a strategy is to understand the current situation, including the behaviors of different species, whether their habitats are expanding or shrinking, and how climate and geographical conditions are changing.

As for collecting data on the Earth, the NTT Group has already released AW3D, the world's first digital three-dimensional map representing the elevation of all the land on the planet's surface in five-meter increments. It uses high-resolution satellite images from the Japan Aerospace Exploration Agency (JAXA) and U.S.-based Maxar Technologies, which operates the world's most advanced satellites, to reveal the true appearances of the Earth in fine detail, from urban areas to mountainous regions that are largely inaccessible to people on the ground. Before we take action to create a sustainable society, we must analyze the Earth's condition with data such as this digital three-dimensional map.

The problem of faster power consumption due to the growth of generative AI

Collecting and analyzing such a massive amount of data to help address social issues will also require a corresponding increase in power usage. For example, the Green IT Initiative that Japan's Ministry of Economy, Trade and Industry launched in December 2007 predicted that in the future, IT equipment will consume approximately five times more power in 2025 compared to 2006, rising to around twelve times more in 2050.

Furthermore, the rapid development of AI has accelerated the growth in power consumption in recent years. In particular, the creation of a large-scale language model (LLM), which is central to generative AI, requires a tremendous amount of computational processing. Some recent generative AIs possess tens of billions of parameters. Building a language model on this scale reportedly requires 1,300 megawatt-hours of power, which exceeds the amount of power a 1,000-megawatt nuclear power plant can generate in one hour (see Chapter 4). What's more is that a large-scale language model needs yet more power to perform regular updates. At this rate, our society will require an unimaginable amount of power.

It is within this context that Google revealed in its July 2024 annual environmental report that the company's greenhouse gas emissions have increased by around 50 percent over a four-year period. Google attributed this to the expansion of the data centers it needs to develop Gemini, its proprietary generative AI. The same trend can be seen at other American companies such as Amazon and Microsoft, as they build data centers for their generative AIs, too.

If power consumption continues to rise along the current trajectory, restrictions on its use may one day force us to suspend technological innovation. Or, before that happens, global warming may progress to the point where the planet becomes too hot for humans and other living things to survive. Unless we dramatically reduce the amount of power we use, our society will eventually cease to function.

Should we halt technological innovation when a problem comes up?

What, then, are we to do? Should we slow the pace of technological innovation to consume less power? Should we abandon AI, give up on new development, and go back to the "good old days"?

No. Slower innovations in technology will certainly not solve the problem. With eight billion people living on this planet, we cannot avoid putting a heavy burden on it. However, technology could mitigate that strain. In fact, history shows that technological innovations have improved humanity's impact on the global environment.

Let's take air pollution, for example. It was a problem for Japanese society in the 1960s. People in this country in their forties or older may recall the daily "photochemical smog" warnings in the summer. However, thanks to innovations such as better exhaust gas purification technology and the shift from coal and oil to electrical energy, the air quality in Japan's cities has improved considerably.

The swift spread of renewable energy is also a gift of technological progress. In both Japan and around the world, the cost of generating renewable energy such as solar and wind power has fallen dramatically over the past decade. In certain regions, it is now even less expensive than power from fossil fuels. We are in the midst of a rapid transition from energy that is obtained by mining and burning the Earth's limited resources, to more environmentally friendly and sustainable energy sources from the sun and the wind.

Ultimately, humanity cannot halt the march of progress. The path we should choose at this point is to encourage technological innovation while simultaneously working to address the social issues that arise from it. Perhaps what we need in this era is a paraconsistent logic by which we can simultaneously achieve conflicting goals that a dualistic approach would rule out. To not use something simply because it will require more data and power is not the way to true well-being. Data and power are essential to human well-being. IOWN could be the key to reconciling our conflicting needs for well-being and a livable planet.

Light: the way to use less power

IOWN's main distinguishing trait is that it replaces electrical signals with optical ones. What, then, are the benefits from replacing electricity with light?

One advantage of optical technology is that light travels incredibly fast. As everyone knows, it is the fastest thing in the universe. Nothing can surpass it. By fully harnessing the properties of light, we can transmit immense amounts of data at high speeds with little latency.

Another advantage of light is, as we have already discussed, its ability to conserve energy. When you try to transmit large amounts of data with electrical signals, it generates considerable heat. That heat is converted from the electricity, which means that some of the energy is lost. This is why data centers with numerous servers and network devices, for example, require a substantial amount of electricity to power the cooling equipment that counters the massive quantity of heat produced.

On the other hand, when transmitting and processing data with optical signals, much less heat is generated. By capitalizing on this property, we can gradually replace our current communications infrastructure that employs electrical signals, from long-distance networks to internal computer wiring, with optical signals that will vastly bring down power consumption.

Roadmap of Advancements Toward 100x Better Power Efficiency

What effect can we expect from actually replacing electricity with light?

Latency is already down to 1/200th

For IOWN, we have set the following specific targets relative to current electricity-based systems: power savings through 100 times better power efficiency (i.e., one hundredth the power usage), and communications performance with 125 times better capacity and one two-hundredths the latency. Given light's potential, we believe these figures are fully achievable. In fact, APN IOWN 1.0, the first network service with the technology platform, has already achieved the latency target (Figure 0-3).

IOWN's development will proceed in stages, beginning with international networks, moving on to shorter-range connections between boards within devices, followed by connections between integrated circuits (i.e., chips), and finally to the world of optical semiconductors within chips. The platform's first version, IOWN 1.0, is a dedicated line service that converts all long-distance transmission routes, such as those between cities, to optical

Figure 0-3 – Latency Already Down to 1/200th

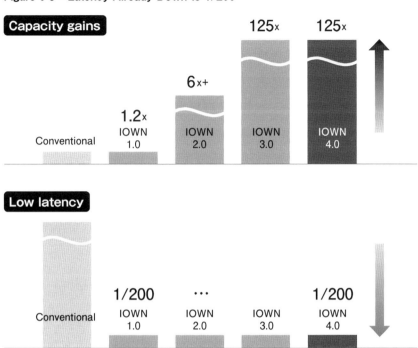

communications. It is called the All-Photonics Network (APN) (Figure 0-4).

The difference between this and conventional fiber-optic services is that communications along the entire line, from end to end, use optical signals. Many lines providing internet connections today already use optical fiber. You may very well have one running to your home. The process employed by current optical fiber services, however, involves converting electrical signals to optical ones at relays and switches along the route, then reconverting them to electrical signals after transmission. Every signal conversion consumes

Figure 0-4 – All-Photonics Network (APN) Conceptual Diagram

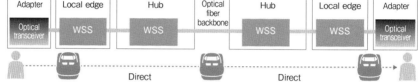

power and inevitably causes latency.

IOWN 2.0 to connect boards with light at Expo 2025 Osaka, Kansai, Japan

An announcement on the commercialization of IOWN 2.0 will coincide with the 2025 Osaka, Kansai Expo. In addition to further boosting APN efficiency, IOWN 2.0 will connect boards inside computers (servers, to be exact) with light, thereby applying optical technology along shorter distances between components. This should enhance power efficiency by thirteen times in the network and eight times in the server (Figure 0-5).

In 2029, we will achieve even greater performance with IOWN 3.0. In this phase, miniaturization will progress enough to replace the electricity

Figure 0-5 – Boards Optically Connected with IOWN 2.0 at Expo 2025 Osaka, Kansai, Japan

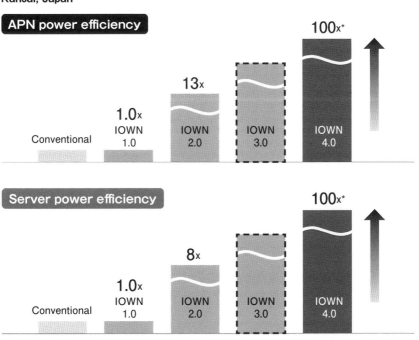

* Power efficiency for all photonics systems, including the APN, servers, etc.

in communications between a board's chips with light. This will increase the capacity by up to 125 times compared to electrical signals, which is our ultimate capacity target for IOWN. The power efficiency at this point will depend on the extent to which optical technology is applied to a given device, but computer components will consume power approximately twenty times more efficiently than they do now.

The next challenge for 2032 and beyond will be optical semiconductors capable of optical communications within chips. This will involve replacing

Figure 0-6 – 100x Power Efficiency from Optical Intrachip Signals with IOWN 4.0 (APN and Server)

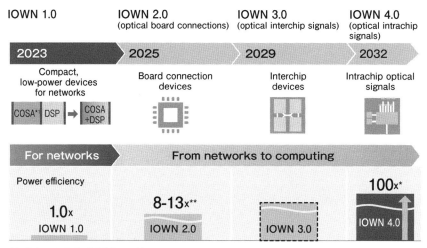

*1. Coherent Optical SubAssembly
* Power efficiency for all photonics systems, including the APN, servers, etc.
** Varies by specific APN and server device

the electricity conventionally used in computing with light. When this happens, IOWN will be one hundred times more power-efficient, thus achieving our ultimate goal for the technology platform (Figure 0-6).

Computers and networks use power one hundred times more efficiently. That sounds like a dream, but we've seen that light can make this technologically feasible. And we believe that working toward this achievement is our mission at the NTT Group, as a leading global technology company with extensive experience researching optical technology.

Introduction: A Light of Hope for Global Sustainability

Co-creation with Partners

The NTT Group has spent many years researching optical fiber and other optical technologies. Our knowledge and experience are substantial in this field, where we are proud to be one of the world's leaders. However, the IOWN Initiative involves a broad range of disciplines and it would be impossible for a single company to cover all aspects of its development and promotion. We believe we can do this through cooperation with numerous partners, including telecommunications companies like NTT, as well as network equipment manufacturers, software developers, chipmakers, and companies that will become IOWN service users. Through co-creation with a variety of partners, the technology's development will accelerate, new ideas will emerge, and we can reach our goal of a sustainable society sooner.

Establishment of the IOWN Global Forum in the United States

In January 2020, NTT, Intel, and Sony (now the Sony Group) established the IOWN Global Forum, an international non-profit organization. It is based in the United States to encourage participation by companies and organizations from across the globe, not just within Japan.

More than four years have passed since its launch, and as of September 2024, the forum's membership has grown to over 150 companies and organizations, far exceeding initial expectations. Members includes

American leaders in AI, such as Microsoft and NVIDIA, as well as Google, which operates large data centers. Each is adding their unique perspective to contribute to IOWN's advancement.

When we talk about IOWN being a game changer, the question we sometimes get is: "But how will you compete against GAFA?" Perhaps the people who ask this imagine a battle playing out between the internet and IOWN, with this new technology going up against those big tech companies that wield the internet to assert their hegemony. That, however, is not an accurate understanding of the situation. IOWN is meant to coexist with the internet. This technology is not intended as a competitor or replacement. Rather, the GAFA companies will become our partners in promoting IOWN.

Each of those companies operates many huge data centers, which poses a challenge due to ballooning power consumption. Therefore, we will become partners who think together about how to use IOWN for efficiency gains and to create a sustainable society. Of course, we will still compete against each other in certain sectors, but IOWN is something we will promote together, along with individual users and other stakeholders.

Incredibly lower power consumption will contribute to planetary sustainability

Achieving sustainability for people and the planet is a central part of NTT's business. Part of this effort is our collaboration with partners around the world to promote IOWN. Within the NTT Group, we are also taking the initiative in advancing efforts to reduce our power consumption with IOWN ahead of its broader implementation.

In September 2021, we produced the "NTT Green Innovation toward 2040", our environmental energy vision that sets the goal of achieving group-wide carbon neutrality by 2040. The new Medium-Term Management Strategy mentioned at the beginning of this chapter also declares a net-zero target. NTT is a telecommunications company with many businesses that consume a large amount of power, such as the mobile phone and data center businesses. At the end of 2013, the NTT Group was using 8.3 billion kilowatt-hours of power a year.

This accounts for just under 1 percent of Japan's total power usage. Our current estimates are that our power consumption will double to around 16 billion kilowatt-hours by 2040. Therefore, we are working through group company NTT Anode Energy to expand our renewable energy generation with wind power and other sources. This already puts us on track to achieve our group-wide target of introducing around 8 billion kilowatt-hours of renewables to our energy sources by 2030 (Figure 0-7). In combination with the energy-savings from IOWN and other initiatives, this effort will eventually allow us to meet our goal of using 100 percent renewable energy by 2040.

In this context, we have drawn up a plan to achieve carbon neutrality for our expected power usage in 2040 by reducing power usage 55 percent through IOWN and other energy-conservation measures, while adding renewable energy sources to cover the remaining 45 percent. Figure 0-8 shows this as a chart with greenhouse gas emissions along the vertical axis. As you can see, IOWN's power savings will account for 45 percent of the reduction. This technology platform will be an essential piece of the puzzle

Figure 0-7 – NTT Group Power Usage Trends and BreakDown

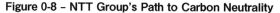

Figure 0-8 – NTT Group's Path to Carbon Neutrality

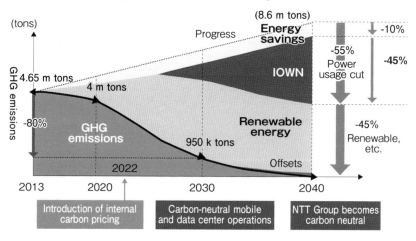

for making society carbon neutral.

We believe NTT will also serve as a useful model for many other companies seeking to achieve carbon neutrality. This is the reduced power consumption you can expect from using IOWN, a technology with the potential to become a veritable light of hope for creating a sustainable future for all companies, users, and indeed, for humanity.

That is why we wish to win the endorsement of as many partners as possible and together take on the challenge of furthering IOWN's development and use.

[Chapter 1]

Commercial IOWN
in Action

Initial Impact of Spread

The first mention of IOWN at a U.S.-Japan summit

In April 2024, Japanese Prime Minister Fumio Kishida paid an official visit to Washington, D.C., where he held a summit with U.S. President Joe Biden. Their meeting resulted in the release of a document titled "United States-Japan Joint Leaders' Statement: Global Partners for the Future." The fact sheet released at that time mentioned IOWN. Below is the relevant section.

"We welcome robust U.S.-Japan private sector cooperation, especially in next-generation semiconductors and advanced packaging. U.S. and Japanese companies are exploring the wide range of possibilities available through optical semiconductors through partnerships like the [Innovative Optical and Wireless Networks (IOWN) Global Forum]."

From the very beginning, we have been promoting the IOWN Initiative by involving companies from around the world. That is because, for the sake of our planet's future, we believe it requires global cooperation to share its vision, rather than being confined to the NTT Group or just Japan. Given that approach, there is great significance in the Japanese and U.S. governments referring to the IOWN Global Forum and the potential of optical semiconductors in official documents, as well as welcoming collaborative promotion of the initiative in Japan and the United States. This event also demonstrated that IOWN is already gaining momentum as an important area of technology that will impact the business of numerous companies.

The long-awaited launch of commercial services

As covered in the Introduction, the NTT Group began providing APN IOWN 1.0, the first commercial service under the IOWN Initiative, in March 2023. That was approximately four years after the IOWN Initiative was announced in May 2019. It was the moment when commercial IOWN at last became a reality. The All-Photonics Network (APN) is a new communications network that employs optical signals along all sections of a transmission route. Because each user accesses only specific optical wavelengths within a section of the route, the network is unaffected by congestion, allowing for the steady sending and receiving of large amounts of data. It is like having your own private expressway, where you never have to worry about traffic jams, even during holiday travel seasons.

Another of IOWN's features is the incredibly low latency, as there is no conversion between optical and electrical signals anywhere along the transmission route. Conventional optical fiber networks require conversion between optical and electrical signals at certain points along a transmission route, which inevitably causes latency. However, because an APN uses optical fiber along all network routes, it enables ultra-low latency with delays that are only one two-hundredths of that in conventional networks. This figure represents the physical limit imposed by the speed of light, the speed which IOWN transmissions come very close to reaching.

Unnoticeable ultra-low latency for music and sports

Here's an example to illustrate what it is like to experience this low latency. In February 2023, before the launch of IOWN commercial services, we put on a concert, "Innovation x Imagination: Futuristic Concert Resonating Beyond Distances II." It was an undertaking in which we used an APN to connect four venues across Japan, located in Tokyo, Osaka, Kanagawa, and Chiba, where musicians would perform together live. When the music started, every instrument was in perfect sync. The performance sounded so brilliant that a listener would never suspect the musicians were playing so far away from each other.

The transmissions traveling at the speed of light along optical fiber cables covering the approximately seven hundred kilometers between Tokyo and Osaka will have a latency of about four milliseconds. Since it takes another four milliseconds to convert the sound and video into signals and back again, the concert experienced a total latency of around eight milliseconds.

This latency is nearly the same as that from sound traveling a distance of three meters. In other words, the sound of a piano played in Tokyo reaches the ears of a fellow performer in Osaka before it reaches an audience member seated ten meters away from that piano. When you think about it like that, you realize just how astonishingly low IOWN's latency is.

In March 2024, we further extended the distance to hold a similar concert simultaneously in Tokyo and Kanazawa. The two venues were connected by approximately one thousand kilometers of optical fiber (Figure 1-1). This was the longest connection yet for an APN demonstration. The performance

Figure 1-1 – Network Configuration for Concert in Tokyo and Kanazawa

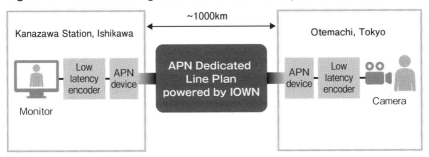

between Kanazawa Junior Jazz Orchestra JAZZ-21 in Kanazawa and the violinist in Tokyo were so in sync that listeners couldn't help but sway to the music.

The potential applications for this technology platform extend well beyond music. At the Interop Tokyo communications network exhibition in June 2023, a demonstration presented a virtual table tennis match with an opponent in a distant location in Japan connected by IOWN. Around one hundred kilometers of optical fiber connected Makuhari Messe in Chiba to an NEC plant in Abiko, Chiba Prefecture via an APN. Footage of players captured with 4K cameras against backgrounds was transmitted in real time, allowing them to play table tennis against each other in a virtual space. Their rallies were shown on monitors at the exhibition venue. Attendees cheered for the players, who seemed locked in a real-world faceoff with no hint of latency in their feeds.

By making the most of IOWN's ultra-low latency, we can expect to see applications that stretch the imagination in a wide range of fields in addition to entertainment like music and sports, such as business and medicine. What future awaits us? The possibilities abound.

Creating the first international IOWN APN connection

APN applications are certainly not limited to Japan. In fact, international connections are underway. In August 2024, NTT and major Taiwanese telecom service provider Chunghwa Telecom established the world's first international APN connection by building an optical network linking Japan and Taiwan over a distance of some three thousand kilometers, with a transmission speed of one hundred gigabits per second (Figure 1-2).

Despite carrying large amounts of data over a long distance, the communications network has a largely constant latency of about seventeen milliseconds each way. A conventional internet connection between the two locations has a latency of between two hundred and five hundred

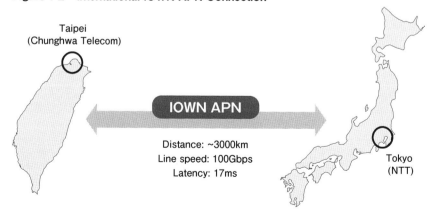

Figure 1-2 – International IOWN APN Connection

milliseconds due to network equipment converting between optical and electrical signals. That means the APN can reduce latency to as low as about one-thirtieth that of a conventional network.

Another noteworthy fact is that this first-ever international APN connection was made possible by interconnecting equipment from different manufacturers who support the Open All-Photonic Network Functional Architecture (OAA), a technical configuration the IOWN Global Forum developed. This achievement should provide considerable encouragement to companies around the world as they build APNs.

At the international APN connection ceremony held in both Taiwan and Japan (Figure 1-3), the network's effectiveness was demonstrated through

Figure 1-3 – International APN Opening Ceremony Held by Connecting Taiwan and Japan

a chorus celebrating the creation of this first-of-its-kind international connection, with video and audio relayed between the two venues. At that time, Chunghwa Telecom Chairman Shui-Yi Kuo commented on the technology's future development, saying, "We will work closely with NTT to develop innovative IOWN technology, establish many use cases for the IOWN APN, and contribute to a prosperous society by encouraging its adoption worldwide."

NTT's collaboration with Chunghwa Telecom, with their outstanding technology and extensive global business experience, to create an international APN connection with IOWN will accelerate the development of IOWN technology and the rollout of services in both Taiwan and Japan, such as data backup and replication.

This international APN connection also produced an opportunity to expand the use of APNs around the world. In the future, we believe international APN connections will contribute to solutions to many issues that different industries and companies face. We plan to continue collaborating with various players to expand international APNs.

Training Programs Kick Off

In the eighteen months since IOWN businesses have rolled out since the commercial service launch, many media outlets, including TV and newspapers, have provided coverage of the technology and the U.S.-Japan summit mentioned at the beginning of this chapter. Meanwhile, future IOWN professionals are already in training.

Training program to produce IOWN pros

In addition to traditional network technology and IT skills, getting the most out of IOWN requires knowledge and competencies in new domains to, for example, put the platform's ultra-low latency to good use. Realizing this, there are now companies wanting to train IOWN professionals ahead of the technology's widespread adoption.

Among these companies there is AKKODiS Consulting, a company that provides technical support and human resource development services. They established an IOWN Promotion Office in February 2024 to train IOWN professionals and create new employment opportunities, then joined the IOWN Global Forum the following month. AKKODiS Consulting has also been a proactive partner in promoting the IOWN Initiative.

Naohiko Morimoto, the Prime Account Director and General Manager at AKKODiS Consulting's IOWN Promotion Office, explains why his company has been so eager to help. "We expect IOWN will help Japan to break free of its stagnation and create opportunities for us to be competitive on the global stage again." The company believes that the key to the IOWN Initiative's success will be how many project managers with the right technical and business perspectives they can train and develop. Hence their focus on developing training and certification programs.

In July 2024, AKKODiS Consulting began providing IOWN Initiative Basic Training for businesspeople and engineers to obtain fundamental knowledge about the social context necessitating IOWN technology, its structural components, and how it will change the future.

We can expect to see more IOWN professionals with specialized knowledge and skills in the future. As we've seen in examples such as live music and sports, these professionals could become indispensable across a wide range of industries.

Why IOWN Is a Game Changer

From the telephone to the internet, and now IOWN

How, then, will IOWN change society? To learn that, let us briefly review the history of communication networks, from the telephone to the internet and now IOWN.

As you may know, NTT, or Nippon Telegraph and Telephone Corporation, was originally a telephone company. We put up telephone poles across Japan to build a telephone network. Most of our profits from that time came from telephone services.

Telephone services were premised on a single line providing a dedicated communications channel between the people on either end of a call. You can think of it like connecting a pair of cups with a piece of yarn. During the call, no one else would have access to the line. That meant if someone else tried to call you, they couldn't connect to you and would hear a busy signal. This type of one-on-one telecommunication, called "circuit switching," allowed for stable communication without interference from other people's calls.

Major change to that infrastructure came with the spread of the internet in the 1990s. On the internet, multiple users share a single line. The way it works is through a system called "packet communication," which divides the data into "packets" of a certain size before transmission. This allows a single line to send a mix of different data. This shared use system is why we can send an e-mail with the press of a button, without wondering whether we'll receive a busy signal, which we would get if we call a phone number to initiate a one-on-one conversation with someone already on another call.

Another impact of these shared lines on the internet is a dramatic drop in the cost of communication. You may recall the phone bills one would receive in the days before the internet. Those charges were determined by distance, and the farther away two people on a call were, the more expensive it was. For example, a long-distance call between Tokyo and Osaka would cost several hundred yen for three minutes, and an international call for the same duration would set you back several thousand yen. But now, you can talk to someone on the other side of the world for free over the internet.

The internet and a seismic shift in society

By enabling connections between anyone, the internet has fundamentally altered society, from our lifestyles to corporate business models. We can now access all kinds of information online and easily communicate with people anywhere in the world with email and chat tools.

What further amplified the internet's power was the arrival of the smartphone. With these palm-sized internet-connected devices we carry around at all times, the ability to connect anytime, anywhere, 24 hours a day, 365 days a year, is a capability we now take for granted.

For example, you can purchase music or a movie online and consume it immediately, find and book a table at a restaurant with good reviews on a food website, or search for information on a topic that piques your interest and instantly get an answer. Now that smartphones and the internet have permeated every aspect of our existence, it can be difficult to remember what life was like before the internet.

Signs of the internet's limitations

However, even the internet has its limits. Packet communication, the fundamental mechanism of the internet, is not stable because many people use the network simultaneously. It is a "best-effort" type of communication in that its quality varies according to the line's conditions at the time, while congestion affects transmission speed and latency. You have to actually send data before you can find out how fast it will travel and how much latency there will be.

In some cases, the connection may cut off before a transmission finishes. Have you ever used a free calling app and gotten cut off in the middle of a call? This would have been unthinkable when telephone calls were the norm, but it is not at all unusual when using an internet-based calling apps. So long as you are communicating over the internet, it is only natural to expect some amount of delay in sending data, along with unstable speeds. That is the standard we have come to accept.

It has been about three decades since the internet became widespread. At some point, it influenced our expectations toward communications, without us realizing it. When we come up with new ideas or develop new businesses, we may be unwittingly basing them on our assumptions about the internet's limitations.

IOWN will bring time synchronization back to the network

The IOWN APN provides added value that the internet today cannot. One crucial example is time synchronization. This functionality allows systems and devices connected to a network to share accurate time. It enables accurate time synchronization between the sender and recipient at either end of a network.

Smartphones and computers may seem like they are synchronized over the internet, but a closer look reveals discrepancies we can measure in milliseconds. This poses challenges when using the internet in ways that demand precisely synchronized time, such as remote control of mobility solutions. For example, if a command to step on the brake at a certain moment is carried out at a slightly different moment, remotely operating an automobile would be a dangerous proposition.

Furthermore, because an APN uses a wavelength serving as a single dedicated line shared between the sender and recipient, congestion is not an issue, just like with an old-fashioned telephone. Transmission distance may cause very slight latency of a few milliseconds, but that latency is constant. Synchronizing time with an APN enables transmissions with even more precise timing so they can meet the rigorous demands for remote control and automatic driving features in mobility solutions.

Accurate time synchronization will allow us to use these networks in ways that were difficult on the internet. Many other areas beyond mobility solutions require accurately synced time, such as telesurgery and remote control of construction machinery. A more familiar example is in esports, where synchronized time is crucial as players compete against each other in computer games. To ensure fair competition, all players must start at exactly the same time, no matter where their location is.

Conversations between AI chatbots also need accurate time synchronization

If we broaden our perspective yet further, we can see that AI, which looks set to play an increasingly important role in the future, will also require accurately synced time. That is because we can expect that we will eventually link up multiple AIs so they can collaborate.

We envision a future where AIs work together and engage in conversations with each other. (See Chapter 4 for further details.) Time synchronization will be crucial when forming teams of collaborative AIs.

For example, computers quickly execute processes at speeds of millions or tens of millions of cycles per second. Therefore, it is important that we make the most of this speed so the AIs can converse with each other efficiently. In a conversation where you don't know when comments are made, if you ask a question about a previous comment when someone has already added a new comment you aren't aware of yet, it's hard for the discussion to progress very far. AIs will find it impossible to collaborate quickly in such a setting. But if we can give them accurately synchronized time, then they will recognize when each comment has been made. A network with such highly accurate time synchronization will allow the AIs to work together much more efficiently and very quickly.

IOWN, which comes with advanced features such as accurate time synchronization, is a new network opening up possibilities beyond those enabled by the internet. By taking IOWN into account to expand your ideas beyond the internet's limitations, you could hit upon new business innovations.

The economic logic of the internet: a double-edged sword

Let us examine one further difference between the internet and IOWN: the internet's open nature. A single set of rules, the TCP/IP protocol, underpins the entire internet. Because all network devices use the same protocol, their prices are much lower than they otherwise would be. And the more widespread those devices become, the greater this effect. From an economic standpoint, this makes the internet a wonderful framework.

However, it also comes with drawbacks. Open protocols mean that outside observers can see how information flows. This is not very secure. The internet's openness is one reason for the frequency of cyberattacks targeting companies and states these days.

In the IOWN network, however, users share a single dedicated line (or wavelength, to be precise). This allows them to use any protocol they like, according to their needs. And the use of more advanced protocols for different uses such as military, medical, and manufacturing communications can further enhance security.

Society today largely operates according to the rules of the internet. The internet, which anyone can use at any time, has had a huge impact on society. However, it is now time to adopt a more imaginative approach toward the structure of services, business, and society, and to contemplate how we can overcome the internet's limitations. IOWN can be the network underlying this shift.

It all started with a research paper published in 2019

Let us look at why the IOWN Initiative came about in 2019.

APNs will convert all network signals to optical ones. However, so that the IOWN platform can also bring these optical signals to the connections between boards, as well as communications between chips and within individual chips, it requires photonics-electronics convergence technology to replace the electrical signals in some of the electronic circuits to optical signals.

On April 15, 2019, NTT announced research results representing a breakthrough in photonics-electronics convergence technology in British scientific journal Nature Photonics. There had been more than two decades of research into technology to integrate light into parts of electronic circuits, but at the time, the size of the devices and their power consumption were too large for practical use. However, NTT's research on the subject succeeded in cutting power usage by 94 percent compared to conventional designs, paving the way for the practical application of photonics-electronics convergence technology.

By bringing photonics-electronics convergence inside computers, in addition to communication networks, we can achieve a new level of computing that is more than an extension of today's technology. If we can achieve one IOWN goal by multiplying the power efficiency of computers around the world by one hundred times, we will make a tremendous contribution toward achieving the Paris Agreement's global goal of achieving carbon neutrality by 2050.

According to the IOWN roadmap, IOWN 4.0, which will launch as early as 2032, will bring light-based signals inside chips through optical semiconductors. In the future, smaller IOWN optical semiconductors could be embedded into personal devices such as smartphones.

Smartphones that are one hundred times more power efficient might only need to recharge once a year. Or perhaps we could provide these devices with sufficient power by installing small solar panels in them or even generating their power from the heat of our bodies, thus eliminating the need for recharging at all.

Although the miniaturization of photonics-electronics convergence devices so they can fit inside smartphones still requires much research and development, the technical path toward achieving that reality is at least becoming clearer. The 2019 paper that inspired the IOWN Initiative was of great significance for making a major contribution to the creation of a sustainable society through low power consumption.

Redefining Data Centers

While IOWN technology may come to our smartphones at some point in the future, the area where it is likely to effect major change now is data centers. Although most of us do not directly interact with data centers, they are integral to providing many of the search engines, cloud services, music and video streaming platforms, and generative AI tools we use on a daily basis.

The issue of where to build data centers

Data centers are typically large buildings that resemble warehouses. The trend in recent years has been for ever bigger data centers that require more and more land to build on. Inside these buildings are rows of thousands or tens of thousands of computers called servers, each of which is connected to a network.

IOWN has the potential to solve two problems that data centers face. One of those relates to their location.

Demand for cloud and other services has been growing as of late, necessitating the construction of more data centers. Ideally, a new data center should be located as close as possible to existing ones to avoid significant latency in server connections between them. Therefore, if, for example, you already have a data center in central Tokyo and you want to build another, it should be within a thirty-five-kilometer radius of that existing data center.

The problem is a shortage of suitable land in urban areas for large data centers, while people living in residential districts near urban cores have voiced their opposition to the construction of these facilities in their neighborhoods. These factors make securing land for data centers increasingly difficult.

Another big problem is procuring the necessary electricity. The key to building more data centers is finding sources of power to draw upon. For example, if a data center has thousands or tens of thousands of servers, it will use an enormous amount of electricity. The limited number of locations with good conditions for sourcing this much power makes location a particularly vexing issue.

Proof-of-Concept test along 100km between Yokosuka and Mitaka

IOWN will help address these issues. Using APNs for communications between data centers will significantly reduce the latency arising from the distance between them, allowing for the construction of additional data centers within twice the distance, meaning a radius of seventy kilometers. In our Tokyo example, this would mean that Chiba Prefecture and the Miura Peninsula would become possible locations, expanding potential data center construction to suburbs with more land and electricity supply to spare (Figure 1-4).

To verify the effectiveness of using an APN for communications between data centers, NTT conducted a Proof-of-Concept test in February 2024 that connected the approximately one hundred kilometers between Yokosuka in

Figure 1-4 – APNs Vastly Expand the Range of Suitable New Data Center Locations

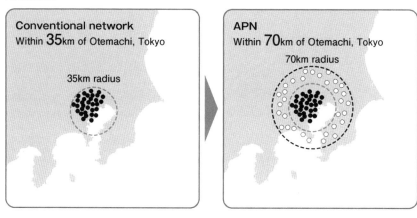

Figure 1-5 – PoC Test with APN Connecting Yokosuka, Kanagawa and Mitaka, Tokyo

GPU: graphics processing unit, DB: database, NFS: network file system

Kanagawa Prefecture and Mitaka in Tokyo with an APN. Servers in Mitaka housed the main components of tsuzumi, NTT's large language model for AI, while data for machine learning was stored in Yokosuka. The experiment involved transmitting the data to Mitaka at high speed to conduct machine learning (Figure 1-5). The test results showed that compared to when the data and tsuzumi servers were placed alongside each other, machine learning's efficiency was degraded by only 0.5 percent.

In the past, when one needed to process large amounts of data, it was common practice to set up a data center where that data was stored. This was due to slow network speeds and the time it took to transfer data. Using an APN, on the other hand, enables high-speed communications with little latency arising from distance. That makes it easier to set up a data center in a suburban area with plenty of land, to which you can transfer data whenever you need it processed.

IOWN is also undergoing testing in other countries that face the same data center location issues as Japan (Figure 1-6). In April 2024, demonstration tests in the U.K. and the U.S. connected data centers with IOWN APNs so they could operate as if they were a single facility. Major operators have specified a limit of two milliseconds as the maximum latency for connections between data centers in order to treat them as a single entity. These tests confirmed that communications between data centers located approximately eighty-nine kilometers apart could achieve a low latency of no more than one millisecond. Further tests are planned for India and other countries, thus expanding potential uses for IOWN APNs.

In the future, restrictions on CO_2 emissions, overburdened power grids,

Figure 1-6 – PoC Tests Connecting Data Centers in the U.K. and U.S.

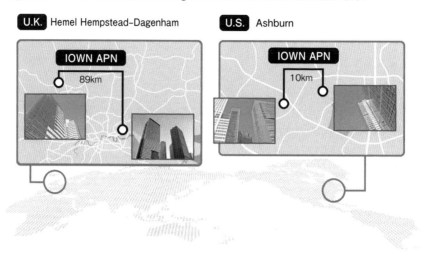

and a lack of land may pose challenges in building new data centers around the world. A number of countries and cities, including Ireland, Germany, Singapore, and the Dutch capital of Amsterdam, which already host data center clusters, have been introducing regulations on new data center construction. Given these circumstances, distributed data centers using IOWN are a promising solution.

Enabling local energy production and consumption

Connecting data centers with IOWN APNs also yields significant energy benefits. The longer the distance over which power is transmitted, the more power is lost along the way. This is why data centers that use large amounts of power should ideally be located as close as possible to power plants.

Figure 1-7 – APN Enabling Local Energy Production and Consumption

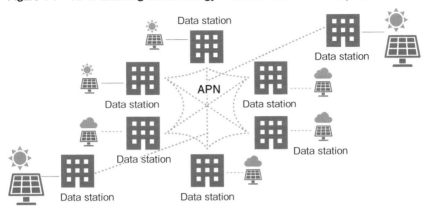

From large centers to small, distributed data stations
Energy is locally produced and consumed

Greater flexibility in selecting data center locations, thanks to APNs, will help reduce energy loss by allowing for their construction closer to power plants, leading to more efficient electricity usage. As a result, APNs could help lower the cost of moving data because they reduce power consumption.

Furthermore, assuming that data can move freely within an APN, we can choose where to process data depending on the energy situation at that time. In Japan, for example, if there are clear skies in Hokkaido today resulting in excess solar power, then one could take advantage of the weather by processing the data there. This flexibility could facilitate local energy production for local consumption, thus preventing waste from curtailment of renewable energy that experiences large swings in generating capacity (Figure 1-7).

The next step: computing

We have so far focused on the future we can open up with IOWN and its APNs for long-distance communications. On the IOWN roadmap, this phase is IOWN 1.0.

But IOWN is not just about connecting different places. In the next step, IOWN 2.0, we plan to use light to replace the electricity in communications over shorter distances. Chapter 2 will examine how in this step, IOWN will employ light to form connections between computer boards and between integrated circuits (i.e., chips).

[Chapter 2]

The Impact of Photonics-Electronics Convergence Devices

Expanding IOWN from Networks to Computing

IOWN is a technology platform that uses optical communications to replace conventional electrical communications for data transmission and processing. Chapter 1 introduced IOWN's features, with a focus on the All-Photonics Network (APN) that connects all routes for long-distance communication between cities and other locations with light. This application lies in the network domain. In the IOWN framework, server infrastructure and digital twin computing, which reproduces reality in a virtual space, will operate on top of APNs (Figure 2-1).

IOWN's applications will also extend into smaller computers through the

Figure 2-1 – The IOWN Framework

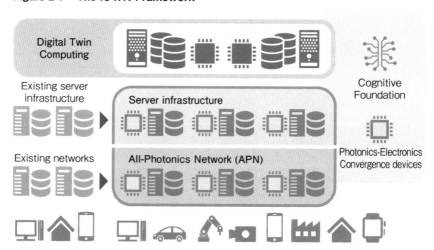

evolution of the photonics-electronics convergence (PEC) devices covered in Chapter 1. This will involve the use of optical semiconductors that will replace electricity with light in (1) the connections between the boards that hold central processing units (CPUs), graphics processing units (GPUs), and memory; (2) between the integrated circuits (i.e., chips), such as CPUs and GPUs, on each board; and (3) the signals traveling inside the chips. In this chapter, we will examine the ways to use IOWN in computing.

Expanding photonics-electronics convergence technology to smaller devices and chips

One key to IOWN's innovations is the photonics-electronics convergence technology that replaces some of the electronic circuits that handle electrical signals with optical signals. Another is Data-Centric Infrastructure (DCI), an information processing platform that allows applications to run effectively on the resources in an optical network. First, as we review the roadmap in terms of the evolution of photonics-electronics convergence devices (Figure 2-2), let's take a look at how IOWN will develop.

Commercialized in 2023, APN IOWN 1.0 is a telecommunications service that, to put it simply, is designed for applications that require communications with extremely high quality and low latency, such as connections between data centers. To achieve this, we use first-generation photonics-electronics convergence devices called PEC-1. These compact, low-power devices for networks each have an area of only a couple square centimeters (Figure 2-3).

Next, IOWN 2.0, which will connect the boards inside computers with light, is coming in 2025. It will use PEC-2, second-generation photonics-

Figure 2-2 – IOWN Roadmap in Terms of Photonics-Electronics Convergence Device Evolution

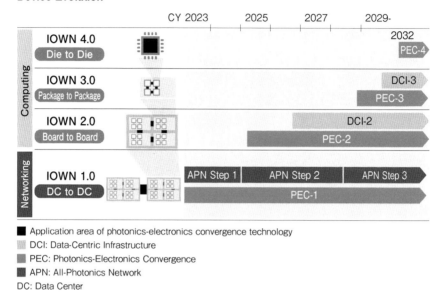

- Application area of photonics-electronics convergence technology
- DCI: Data-Centric Infrastructure
- PEC: Photonics-Electronics Convergence
- APN: All-Photonics Network
- DC: Data Center

Figure 2-3 – The Photonics-Electronics Convergence Device Concept

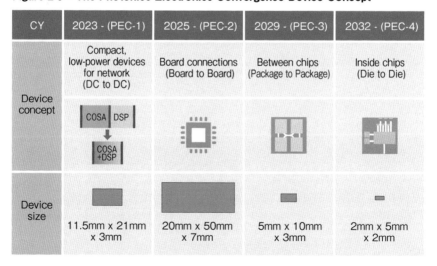

60

electronics convergence devices.

IOWN 3.0 will then further miniaturize the devices with PEC-3 for connections between semiconductor chips. The devices at this stage will be only millimeters scale.

With IOWN 4.0, which we aim to begin developing in 2032, we will attempt to bring optical signals inside chips with PEC-4. IOWN will thus enter the micro realm of optical semiconductors.

On this roadmap, commercial APN services launched with IOWN 1.0's PEC-1. This was the start of the IOWN Initiative. How, then, will PEC-2 in IOWN 2.0 and PEC-3 in IOWN 3.0 change our world? Let's explore them in turn below.

Massive Data Center Efficiency Gains with IOWN 2.0

Efficiency gains at data centers provide a clear example of what IOWN 2.0 can do. Chapter 1 discussed the acute shortage of land for data centers in urban areas, as well as the major problem posed by how much power data centers use. The chapter also introduced a solution, which is to connect data centers with low-latency APNs, thereby providing a wider range of location options in suburban areas with fewer land constraints or regions with abundant sources of renewable energy sources.

IOWN 2.0 will also reduce data centers' power consumption in general because their servers and other devices will require less electricity, while server equipment costs will be much lower. The key to this is optical connections between boards with PEC-2.

Connecting components with light to transcend the "box"

As with the servers in data centers, the components inside a modern computer, such as the CPU, GPU, memory, and storage, are generally placed very close together. This is because the more data in a transmission and the farther it has to travel, the greater the power loss and subsequent power required to complete that transmission. As a result, the components in a modern computer are housed in a chassis, which is a space that resembles a box. Today's data centers contain thousands or even tens of thousands of such boxes, which are connected by network equipment so they can process data.

These servers are connected to each other via a network using the same TCP/IP protocol suite as the internet. In principle, TCP/IP causes latency depending on how much traffic is on the line. For this reason, it is difficult to perform complex processing at high speed across multiple servers. However, a solution has presented itself: direct connections between server boards with light to enable instantaneous communication.

IOWN 2.0 will let us form direct connections between server boards, as well as their memory and other components, with light. This will allow us to efficiently place components a short distance away from the main unit, as communications with optical signals have high speed and capacity, along with low power consumption and power loss, that erase concerns about separation over physical distances.

Furthermore, when we can connect boards and other components with light, we can transcend the use of the conventional "box" and utilize the CPUs, GPUs, memory, and other components across multiple servers all together, rather than confining each processing task to a single server. This flexible shared use of components will also lead to significant reductions in power usage and equipment costs.

One problem with processing data in servers is that we end up wasting their components' capabilities. AI presents a clear example of this. AI training and other processing mostly employs GPUs, which means CPU capabilities are barely tapped. The way servers work today, each one must be equipped with at least one CPU, and if that server's processing is for AI, then the CPU will largely sit idle. When you add up thousands or tens of thousands of server CPUs, the result is more unnecessary power consumption leading to significant loss. By connecting boards with optical signals, IOWN 2.0 will enable shared use of components that could solve problems like this.

Next-generation disaggregated computing

Our term for this system that subdivides and shares the computer components, rather than organizing them into "boxes," is "disaggregated computing" (Figure 2-4). The idea is to disaggregate, or "subdivide," the computers.

As mentioned above, while AI processing makes little use of CPUs, it is very GPU-intensive. This is a scenario where disaggregated computing will allow you to transcend the "boxes" and bundle numerous GPUs for use when you need them.

Figure 2-4 – The Disaggregated Computing Concept

(a) Conventional server configuration

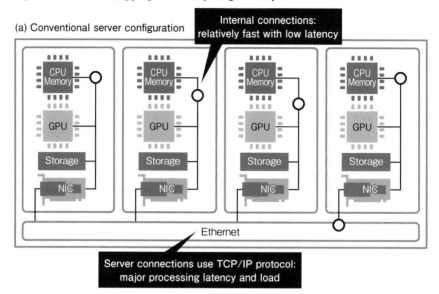

(b) Disaggregated computing

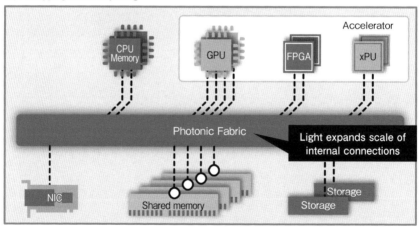

Rack-scale computing transcends the "box"
Consider original physical configurations, logic configurations, and control methods to fully leverage rack-scale computing

Physical configuration   Logic configuration   Control method

NIC: Network Interface Card
FPGA: Field Programmable Gate Array

Disaggregated computing is also effective in cases where the processing load changes according to the time of day. That is because it enables the flexibility to, for example, only start up the components you require while leaving the others off. The advantage would be less power usage.

Disaggregated computing Proof-of-Concept tests already conducted

To test the disaggregated computing Proof-of-Concept, we used real-time analysis of footage from city surveillance cameras. When processing such data to identify a suspect in real time, for example, it is much more challenging task when working with footage of daytime crowds than with nighttime footage with hardly any people. By optimizing our use of components so that we can connect many in the day while leaving more of them off at night, we used 60 to 70 percent less power than conventional computers would.

This is how disaggregated computing enabled by IOWN carries the potential to dramatically change how we utilize servers and substantially reduce power consumption. We are first looking at how we can share the components (i.e., resources) of individual racks, each housing multiple servers, before moving further to share the resources of an entire data center, and then taking it a step further to bundle and share the resources of multiple data centers.

The concept of disaggregated computing holds the most relevance for services and fields where processing a large volume of data is a must, latency is not an option, and processing loads fluctuate significantly. A prime example is the above case of a security service that has to analyze footage from numerous security cameras in real time, a task demanding the processing of considerable data amid wild swings in the load. Meanwhile, Mobility as a Service (MaaS), which involves the coordination of multiple transportation systems to provide optimal mobility services, and automatic driving of vehicles, where even a moment's delay could be fatal, are fields where latency is unacceptable. Disaggregated computing also presents potential for use in a wide range of other areas, including energy management, which involves balancing electricity supply and demand, as well as electronic commerce (EC), live streaming, and gaming.

PEC-2 second-generation photonics-electronics convergence devices will play an important role in bringing this about. Prototypes are already completed and preparations are underway for commercial release in 2025.

The evolution of photonics-electronics convergence devices and Data-Centric Infrastructure (DCI) will expand disaggregated computing to boards and then to chip, which should lead to even greater processing capacity and lower power consumption.

Optical Semiconductor Chips Will Meet the Demands of the AI Era

Let us move on to the next topic. IOWN 3.0, which will enable optical communication between chips, is slated for release in 2029. It will use the PEC-3 third-generation photonics-electronics convergence devices that will be even smaller than their predecessors. To demonstrate the significance of this advancement, we need an understanding of the conditions under which chips (which is shorthand for semiconductor chips or semiconductor integrated circuits) operate.

The "three arrows" for boosting chip performance

The rapid spread of AI has dramatically increased performance demands on semiconductor chips. To meet this demand, the semiconductor chip industry is pursuing technological innovation and performance enhancements along paths we refer to as the "three arrows," which are miniaturization, high-density packaging, and optical communications between chips.

The first arrow: miniaturization

The first arrow is miniaturization. A semiconductor chip is a collection of components called transistors that control electric current. The more transistors, the higher the semiconductor chip's performance. For this reason, the focus of semiconductor chip development has been on how to make each transistors as small as possible and how to pack as many transistors as we can onto a tiny chip. In other words, it has been a quest for an ever-greater degree of integration.

You may have heard of Moore's Law. Over the past fifty years, semiconductor chips have evolved according to this concept.

Moore's Law is a rule of thumb proposed in 1965 by Gordon Moore, one of Intel's founders. In essence, it states that "the number of transistors on an integrated circuit will double every two years." Since it was first espoused, this trend has held up for more than five decades since. This could partly be because Mr. Moore accurately predicted the speed of technological advancements, but is also perhaps attributable to the engineers behind innovations in semiconductors using this law as their objective.

To miniaturize transistors so that more can be mounted onto a semiconductor chip, the line width of its circuits must first be narrow enough to achieve a greater degree of integration. In the past, line widths were measured in micrometers, with 1 micrometer equaling one-thousandth of a millimeter. As miniaturization has progressed, these widths are now measured in nanometers, with 1 nanometer equaling one-millionth of a millimeter, or one-thousandth of a micrometer. Ten-nanometer line widths became commonplace around 2017. Afterward, practical designs were created for 7 nanometers, followed by 5 nanometers, and now 3 nanometers today.

Miniaturization looks set to progress further, as several companies and laboratories have presented roadmaps showing figures such as 1.4 nanometers, 1 nanometers, and 0.7 nanometers. Technologies are now emerging that increase the degree of integration through new transistor configurations, so it is highly likely that Moore's Law will continue to hold true for at least the next ten to fifteen years.

However, as miniaturization progresses, we are approaching physical limits. Ultimately, the line width of a circuit cannot be smaller than an atom, and improving semiconductor performance through miniaturization alone is becoming increasingly difficult due to diminishing returns. This is because as we develop smaller and smaller chips, manufacturing costs rise while gains in performance slow.

The second arrow: high-density packaging

Another trend occurring alongside miniaturization is high-density packaging. Packaging is the process of cutting out and assembling manufactured semiconductor chips. The goal of high-density packaging technology is to achieve higher performance by tightly fitting together multiple semiconductor chips of different types and treating them as if they were one giant chip (Figure 2-5).

Technological development is progressing in areas such as advanced 2D and 3D packaging to vertically stack chips that were previously arranged on a flat surface. This work is facilitating the design of semiconductors with higher performance. By mounting components at the highest possible density and shortening circuits, one can expect higher transfer speeds and lower power consumption.

Figure 2-5 – High-Density Packaging Technology

From horizontal packaging to vertical packaging (2.5D IC, 3D IC)

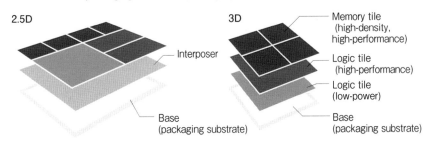

The third arrow: optical communication between chips

The third arrow that contributes to higher performance in semiconductor chips and is the focus of PEC-3, coming with IOWN 3.0, is optical communication between chips.

The farther an electrical signal must travel, the more power it uses. And when the frequency (also known as the clock rate) at which signals are sent is raised to boost transmission capacity, power consumption will grow rapidly, even over short distances, resulting in significant power loss (Figure 2-6). Typical frequencies are ten or twenty gigahertz, but in the near future, we

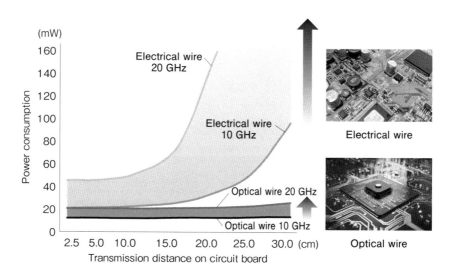

Figure 2-6 – Comparison: Power Consumption from Transmission Distance with Electrical/Optical Signals

can expect to see frequencies of fifty to one hundred gigahertz. With optical signals, on the other hand, power consumption remains fairly constant, even along greater transmission distances, and that power usage experiences no significant gain as the frequency increases.

Let us use the torrid increase in AI processing as an example. The data involved in each processing task is so large that it is too much for a single semiconductor chip, such as a GPU, to handle. Instead, we must connect thousands or tens of thousands of chips and process the data in a distributed manner. However, if the chips are connected with electrical wiring, high-speed transmission will use too much power, and at a certain point, improving performance becomes difficult. In contrast, if we use optical wiring, we can send high-capacity transmissions over long distances, allowing us to connect numerous chips working in tandem at great speed.

Processing for much larger, gigantic tasks means a huge amount of data must be loaded. Even if the processing is accelerated, if the system cannot read the data faster, that extra performance goes to waste. It's the same as a car with a high-performance engine that can't show off what it can do because of a thin fuel hose. This highlights the importance of using optical processing to speed up data transfers between components, such as the CPUs and GPUs that process data and the memory that temporarily stores it.

To outfit computers with the necessary performance as the spread of AI picks up pace, we see it as being essential that we adopt an approach combining the three arrows introduced in this section: miniaturization, high-density packaging, and IOWN's objective of optical communication between chips.

NTT's membrane technology supporting optical advancesments

We have thus far examined how IOWN will change the world with optical technology. But why is it that NTT become a pioneer in technology such as the APN and in photonics-electronics convergence devices like PEC-2 and PEC-3? Let's answer that question now.

This book has already noted that NTT has been researching optical fiber since the 1960s. We are proud that the sum of that work has made us a world leader in optical fiber technology. In fact, it is precisely because of this technology that we can send optical signals over long distances without any loss, thereby enabling long-distance optical communications.

For example, NTT has created a compact, high-efficiency, broadband optical amplifier that, although essential for long-distance optical communication systems, had been considered a challenge for practical use. This technology was later applied to long-distance transmission networks around the world, including trans-Pacific and trans-Atlantic optical undersea cables. NTT was also the first in the world to develop practical applications and establish production techniques for optical fiber with a new type of "holey structure." This innovation, too, is now in use worldwide.

Furthermore, NTT's design technology boasts unparalleled performance in silicon-photonics technology, which employs silicon as the primary ingredient to enable extremely compact optical waveguides and circuits that are suitable for mass production. Silicon-photonics designs are typically created by combining off-the-shelf design components (such as interferometers, multi/demultiplexers, and photoreceivers) prepared by silicon manufacturers called foundries, but NTT creates its designs by developing each component element separately, while optimizing performance down to the physical details by refining waveguide configurations and additive material concentrations.

One result of NTT's optical research was a paper on photonics-electronics convergence that was published in the British scientific journal Nature Photonics, as mentioned in Chapter 1.

What was specifically groundbreaking in this paper was that it described our success in making photonics-electronics convergence devices significantly thinner to serve as membranes. This allowed us to reduce power consumption to one-hundredth of that by photonics-electronics convergence devices produced via conventional methods. Coincidentally, this figure happened to align with our ultimate goal with IOWN of increasing power efficiency by one hundred times, which is the same as using one-hundredth the amount of power. We refer to this process as the "membrane" development method because the devices possess the properties of a membrane. Likewise, the term "membrane photonics" has a broader definition that describes the process of creating photonics-electronics convergence devices by combining two methods. One is the membrane development method. The other is silicon-photonics, to which we apply a proprietary NTT design method as described above (Figure 2-7).

Before the paper's publication in 2019, photonics-electronics convergence technology required so much electricity that it was less power efficient than using electrical signals, so there was no reason to use it. However, the development of membrane photonics in 2019 paved the way for computing

Figure 2-7 – Configuration of Membrane Device Made with Membrane Photonics

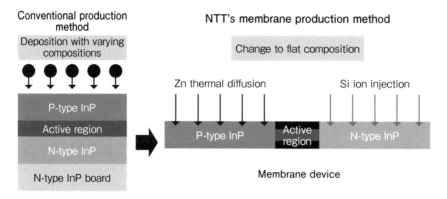

with optical technology.

NTT's strength in optical technology is our corporate group's ability to handle everything from the physical level to the system level (down to materials, component elements, circuits, devices, and systems). This means that from the physical level up, we can create, for example, membrane photonics products with properties optimized for their intended use in a system. And if we can build upon membrane photonics to commercialize PEC-3, which will connect chips with light, we will finally see a one-hundred-fold increase in power efficiency.

NTT, not to mention our country of Japan as a whole, owns an incredible number of patents in many fields related to optical technology, including manufacturing, testing, and materials. In other words, photonics-electronics convergence is an area where Japan's strengths thrive. NTT also owns numerous patents related to PEC-3, which we are developing with the goal of commercialization in 2029. We are proud to be at the forefront of this field, and we hope to continue breaking new ground here in collaboration with our partners.

Developing Photonics-Electronics Convergence Devices In-House and Automating an Art

We have established the technical prospects for creating photonics-electronics convergence devices such as PEC-3 and PEC-4. However, the big question is whether we can develop these innovations beyond pure technology and into commercial products to establish businesses with them.

Provide devices after establishing production and mounting processes

To promote the development and commercialization of photonics-electronics convergence technology, including membrane photonics, we established NTT Innovative Devices as a wholly owned subsidiary in 2023. This company is now working on designing and prototyping photonics-electronics convergence devices and on establishing manufacturing techniques for mass production.

Working with light requires sensitive, sophisticated technology. First, consider the difference between electrical wires and optical fibers. If you were to connect electrical signals, you could send them by simply connecting the wires. However, optical signals travel as waves of light inside optical fibers, and if the fibers are not joined properly, transmissions become impossible. The optical axis running through the center of an optical fiber must be aligned precisely. Even a slight misalignment will cause the light to attenuate, thus preventing the signal's proper transmission.

The process of connecting these optical fibers is called "alignment." Precise alignment is an art. The fact is, we still rely on the expertise of skilled workers.

However, NTT is one of the world's most experienced organizations when it comes to optical fiber, as we have conducted R&D on the technology since its inception. In the field of photonics-electronics convergence devices, we are also working to establish mass production technology as quickly as possible, including maximum automation for the highly skilled techniques in the alignment process.

Building a global ecosystem with many corporate partners

But even if IOWN evolves into something more, the NTT Group alone cannot redefine computing. For example, the semiconductor supply chain is huge, involving an enormous number of companies. You read above that optical technology is a field where Japan excels, but there are many other companies around the world that, just like the NTT Group, are also proactively conducting research in this field.

The IOWN Initiative is by no means only for NTT's sake. It is an ecosystem bringing together members from across the globe who endorse the initiative and pool their expertise to build it. Even if NTT were to accomplish this by itself, equipment costs would not fall, and there would be no guarantees that many companies would adopt IOWN.

Especially when it comes to the development and manufacture of semiconductor chips, the key to success is attracting as many users as possible in advance, which allows one to forecast the large cost reductions that mass production will bring about.

The next chapter will provide a detailed look at how we are recruiting partners for IOWN.

[Chapter 3]

Finding Partners for a Global Platform

The IOWN Global Forum, Founded with Intel and Sony

Thus far, we have introduced how NTT sees IOWN and the company's plans for the technology platform. However, the IOWN Initiative is an incredibly wide-ranging project that the NTT Group cannot promote on its own. From the outset, we have considered recruiting like-minded partners around the world to help us bring the project to fruition.

This is why in January 2020, about seven months after announcing the IOWN Initiative, Intel and Sony (now the Sony Group), the first companies to jump on board with the concept, joined us in establishing the IOWN Global Forum. The organization is headquartered in the United States. NTT Senior Executive Vice President Katsuhiko Kawazoe was appointed as President and Chairperson (Figure 3-1).

Expectations exceeded with over 150 members

We chose to base the organization in the United States because we want IOWN to be worldwide, not just confined to Japan. If we had located it in Japan, IOWN would have been regarded very much as a Japanese standard. However, as we can see from Intel's position as a co-founding member, the concept itself holds appeal to companies across the globe as a collaborative project.

Due in part to our adoption of a global approach from the beginning, over 150 organizations around the world, including renowned companies and

Chapter 3 – Finding Partners for a Global Platform

Figure 3-1 – NTT Senior Executive Vice President Katsuhiko Kawazoe Speaks at the IOWN Global Forum (April 2024)

universities, have joined the IOWN Global Forum as of September 2024, more than four years after its creation (Figure 3-2). When the forum was first established, we defined great success as recruiting five companies in the first year and thirty in the second. There was also talk of setting a goal of one hundred companies by 2030. The figures show, however, that the membership's growth has far outpaced these ambitions, with thirty-nine companies joining in the first year and eighty-eight in the second. Members are from many different regions, including Japan and elsewhere in Asia, as well as the United States and Europe. It very much seems that the forum is attracting far more participants than we had anticipated.

Figure 3-2 – IOWN Global Forum Membership (as of September 2024)

A wide range of companies and organizations from different sectors have become members. In telecommunications, for example, KDDI and Rakuten Mobile from Japan, Orange from France, Chunghwa Telecom from Taiwan, and SK Telecom from South Korea have joined. In semiconductors, in addition to founding member Intel, we have Samsung Electronics and SK Hynix from South Korea, and AI sector darling NVIDIA from the Unites States. Other members include telecom equipment manufacturers such as Ciena and Cisco Systems from the United States. and Nokia from Finland, as well as software manufacturers like U.S.-based Oracle and Red Hat and American data center operators including Microsoft and Google. A broad range of other companies and organizations have also joined the forum, among them being research institutes such as the National Institute of Information and Communications Technology in Japan and the Industrial

Technology Research Institute in Taiwan, universities including the University of Tokyo and Tohoku University, as well as companies from many different sectors such as finance, transportation, chemistry, and broadcasting who are potential IOWN users.

The IOWN Global Forum was formed to ensure that this technology does not become a proprietary standard confined to Japan. Countless times in the past, when Japan has invented outstanding technology, it has quietly disappeared after failing to become mainstream in other countries. IOWN can contribute to achieving global sustainability, but it cannot do so if it remains in Japan alone. It is critical that we make it as open as possible and work with as many partners as we can to develop the technology platform, formulate specifications, and drive standardization.

Weekly meetings ahead of the forum's creation fostered unity

To recruit a greater number of members, we began working on creating the IOWN Global Forum immediately after the IOWN Initiative was announced in May 2019. Reportedly, it typically takes around two years of preparation to launch an international organization like this, but we wanted to recruit members as soon as possible to start spreading this technology, so we laid the groundwork at a rapid pace.

After Intel and Sony agreed to work with NTT on IOWN, the three companies met weekly online and monthly in person to hammer out the details. The locations rotated between Intel's offices in Portland, Oregon, Sony's in New York City, and NTT Research's in Silicon Valley. In January 2020, after about three months of preparation, we could create the IOWN

Global Forum.

After the new forum was announced, we were planning to hold an event at the Mobile World Congress (MWC), one of the world's largest mobile device tradeshows, in Barcelona at the end of February 2020 to give everyone a grand introduction to the IOWN Global Forum. It was around that time, however, that COVID-19 was spreading. As a result, the MWC was canceled just a few weeks before its scheduled start. This cost us an opportunity to promote the IOWN Global Forum we had been working so hard to prepare. Our first gathering of members, slated for Tokyo in April, was also canceled. It was a terribly worrying time that made us wonder if all our work had been for naught.

Documentation produced in online meetings until the first in-person conference in the fall of 2022

However, it turned out that our inability to talk face-to-face was not entirely bad. Meeting online without having to travel has the advantage of allowing for frequent discussions with people located all over the world. Talks proceeded at a fast clip. After meeting online for an hour, the participants could carry out their assigned tasks and then reconvene a couple weeks later for further discussion.

In the IOWN Global Forum's first two years, we wrote and shared a considerable number of technical specifications and other documents. The switch to online conferences may have been one reason why we could produce the documentation with such speed.

For organizations like the IOWN Global Forum that are just starting out, that speed is of the essence. Standardization organizations in the telecommunications usually take their time, often two years or longer, to carefully deliberate over and finalize a single specification. A new organization, however, will see its membership shrink if it does not lead to any results within two years. While it was unfortunate that the forum's creation coincided with the outbreak of COVID-19, we seem to have adapted well in that we quickly produced results.

In its first two years, the IOWN Global Forum operated entirely online. It was in October 2022 that we met in New York to hold our first in-person meeting. We had approximately 150 participants gathered at the venue and around 200 to 300 joining online, making this a hybrid conference. By this time, we had spent about two years discussing matters such as how to produce documents. We knew each other's voices, but not the faces so well, so when speakers went up to the stage to give presentations, we sometimes had no idea who they were until they started speaking in a familiar voice. It was a curious, new experience that is hard to forget.

Dual Focus on Technology and Use Cases

Let's now go into further detail on what the IOWN Global Forum is and what it does. What makes the organization distinct is that it brings together tech companies developing basic technology and writing specifications and user companies interested in leveraging IOWN for their businesses. For this reason, the forum's work focuses on two areas: developing technology and designing use cases.

Tech and user company participation creates a virtuous cycle

The world has many standardization organizations in different fields, as well as user organizations for technologies. However, it is rare to find an organization that encompasses both domains. At the IOWN Global Forum, we believe it is critical that stakeholders in both technological development and use cases join our organization and collaborate.

It seems that many tech companies consider optical technology's integration into networks and computing to be a natural progression. At the forum, participants discuss the technical specifications and standards for their respective fields of expertise.

User companies, meanwhile, are seeking solutions to problems in their own organizations or industries. When they ask the forum whether IOWN can solve a particular problem, tech companies seize the opportunity to pitch ideas for solutions and how to implement them.

This process has had a major positive impact on IOWN technology development and specification writing, as it has given us a clear picture of how exactly the technology will address certain issues that society faces. Indeed, a diverse range of user companies are involved in the forum and are sharing the issues their respective industries confront. Our discussions about numerous specific use cases have identified what users need from the technology, creating a positive feedback loop for technological development[1] (Figure 3-3).

Figure 3-3 – The IOWN Global Forum's Work

Create use cases	Draw up a technical roadmap	Write technical specifications (e.g., architecture, requirements)	Promote & grow (with standardization organizations)

Use cases & applications
(IOWN Global Forum vision, motivating use cases, estimated potential business impacts, technical requirements)

Technical solutions
(reference architecture, protocols, interfaces, specifications)

Smart energy · Smart cities · Smart mobility

Networks (optical/wireless) · Distributed computing

Smart finance · Smart entertainment

Photonics & optoelectronics · Devices, interface terminals

Other use cases & applications

Other technology

Embarking on Proof-of-Concept testing

Next, let's take a look at exactly what kind of technologies we have been discussing.

The IOWN Global Forum has been drawing up a roadmap and furthering action in Phases 1 and 2. During Phase 1, which ran until January 2022, the focus was on determining our approach and planning action, as well as defining our vision, key use cases, and the basic technical framework and issues to examine. Phase 2 followed and concluded in July 2023. During that time, we updated the vision, use cases, and architecture, developed technical specifications and a standard model for implementation, and conducted

Proof-of-Concept (PoC) testing.

A PoC involves verification of ideas and technical specifications with prototypes and tests that determine their feasibility. An example is the real-time analysis of surveillance camera footage described in Chapter 2. This PoC was recognized by the IOWN Global Forum. Connecting computer components with IOWN technology will enable disaggregated computing with greater flexibility in hardware configuration and lower power consumption. This PoC testing has demonstrated that the platform can achieve the intended results.

Let's dig deeper into this PoC. Disaggregated computing was employed for processing the task of detecting humans in 4K footage from eight cameras. The computer components were connected with IOWN photonics-electronics convergence devices serving as switches. To consume less power, we optimized the hardware configuration in use according to changes in the processing power required for detecting people, as the number of people appearing in the footage changes between day and night. The result was 30 percent less power used at night compared to the daytime. And as explained in Chapter 2, the PoC confirmed that this setup consumes approximately 60 to 70 percent less power than a conventional computer configuration would. This was one of seven PoCs selected for Phase 2.

When Phase 3 began in August 2023, we built on these results by focusing on social implementation and business development, with an eye toward commercialization. Our work to carry out the IOWN vision thus continues.

Two Categories of Use Cases to Implement

The IOWN Global Forum's members are considering what kinds of use cases society will need in the future and scrutinizing what sorts of technical specifications those use cases will require. The following section will introduce some of the specific fields where we are attempting to apply IOWN technology.

We classify use cases into two categories: AI communication and cyber-physical systems. The former uses AI to enhance and expand human communication, while the latter is for smart cities that operate autonomously and beyond human capabilities. Let's take a closer look at specific use cases in each category.

AI communication

1. Entertainment

One potential use case for AI communication is entertainment. For example, we could take advantage of the high capacity and low latency in IOWN communications services while using AI to provide spectators at home with a realistic experience that feels like being at a concert venue in person.

Specifically, we could presumably stream high-resolution video and music with views of the performance from any angle. This would enable an immersive experience where viewers can dance alongside the performer or interact with other spectators. We are also considering a mechanism that would allow concert organizers to analyze audience reactions at dispersed venues in real time and use that data to create a virtual concert venue that reflects those reactions.

Spectator sports present a similar use case to live music. We want to create a realistic experience that feels like actually being at a stadium, whether the viewer is at home or in a neighborhood sports bar. Our objective is to deliver an experience where spectators can root for their favorite team alongside other fans in a virtual stadium, and when a goal is scored, the roar of the crowd gathering from around the world reverberates throughout the virtual stadium.

Other use cases under consideration include cloud gaming, where cloud computing does the heavy lifting for processing data, as well as mobile entertainment for people in self-driving cars.

2. Remote operation

The COVID-19 pandemic has made working from home much more common, but many jobs can still only be performed on-site, such as building infrastructure or maintaining machinery. Remote operation is one way IOWN that could be used for such on-site occupations, with worker training being a specific use case we have in mind. Digitalizing the five human senses, such as sight, hearing, and touch, and then transmitting that information in real time will enable immersive remote training and other applications.

When a machine or electronic equipment breaks down, or there is a major system failure, the problem may necessitate support from an expert. In

Chapter 3 – Finding Partners for a Global Platform

situations like these, our idea is to enable rapid diagnosis and response by connecting the site and an expert at a remote location with technologies such as augmented reality (AR).

3. XR navigation

We also wish to explore possibilities in the realm of extended reality (XR), which is a general term for AR and virtual reality (VR), to display information superimposed on the real world.

Imagine, for example, dining at a restaurant. With an XR tool, you could view data displayed over a dish such as its ingredients and calorie count. Or when shopping at a supermarket, you could pick up a food item and virtually experience the flavor and aroma, or even see how it will look after cooking.

Here's another scenario. When you visit a sightseeing spot, you could use an XR device to transmit the sights, sounds, and smells you are experiencing to family members at home thousands of miles away. You could also experience different moments in time by superimposing historical images of the scenery in front of you or simulated images of its future. This XR-based navigation is another promising use case for IOWN.

4. Augmented human abilities

The IOWN Global Forum seeks to create new technologies that augment human abilities. One such proposal is "mind-to-mind communication."

Being able to communicate with people from different cultures is incredibly important for humans. But when there is a misunderstanding, it can often lead to conflict. One reason is that even if you understand the words, you may not fully comprehend the nuances behind them. The purpose of this use case is to enable a new form of communication by translating and expressing not only language, but also the emotions and implicit meanings of the words. One important consideration for this use case is what technical specifications it requires for smooth, latency-free communication.

Another use case is Another Me. This digital avatar records and studies information about you and can even make decisions on your behalf. It is a double of yourself that records all sorts of information for you, such as your everyday communications, health condition, and video game stats, and even makes decisions in certain situations. People today juggle more tasks than they can handle, such as those who struggle to balance work with childcare or nursing care. If you had a double that thought like you and could handle simple tasks in your place, you could devote more time to more important, essential matters.

Cyber-physical systems

1. Area management

In the smart cities that will become more common in the future, various types of sensors collect massive amounts of information. Those devices will include image sensors, high-performance LiDAR, and sensors that use optical fiber. The integration of these sensors to construct a "live 4D map" representing latitude, longitude, altitude, and time will allow for the creation of many different applications. By combining such a map with AI-based incident detection, for example, we could enhance security by predicting crime. These sensors could also be integrated into a system for disaster countermeasures. When the sensors detect an earthquake, the system could automatically operate safety devices in buildings and guide people to optimal evacuation routes.

Other use cases for area management include sophisticated energy management that uses AI to predict energy consumption and allocate optimal power. Another is optimized retail operations that would predict the number of shoppers in malls and then adjust the number of salespeople, inventory, and prices accordingly.

2. Mobility management

IOWN will also play an important role in the rapidly evolving field of mobility. To collect and process the vast amounts of data from sensors and numerous vehicles on roads in real time, IOWN services are a must. Take, for example, automatic driving and remote vehicle operation. These services will need reliable, low-latency communication to collect and process the sensor data from each vehicle and issue instructions to vehicles within a certain time.

It will be important to optimize not just individual vehicles, but also entire transportation systems. Optimizing energy consumption in transportation is a particularly crucial issue to address if we are to create a decarbonized society. One use case would be real-time monitoring of city-wide congestion derived from sensor data. Such a system would allow us to create a digital twin, which is a reproduction of reality in a virtual space. We could then run simulations with the digital twin so as to provide each vehicle with the most energy-efficient route to its destination. Further transportation optimization could be achieved by having vehicle batteries function as temporary power storage devices. To do this, we would have to consider how to integrate those batteries into city power planning. IOWN should prove useful for this task, as well.

3. Industrial management

Spreading digitalization comes with it a need to remotely monitor people and objects in factories, as well as machinery and other equipment. We can see this in Germany's Industry 4.0 policy. An example of this effect can be found on production lines. In order to detect abnormalities at an early stage, analyze their causes, and execute a prompt response, the line must have multiple high-definition surveillance cameras with 4K or 8K resolution, as well as a system that can detect abnormalities by processing the data with AI. To turn such use cases into reality, the IOWN Global Forum is considering the necessary specifications for transmitting and processing the voluminous data from these surveillance cameras in real time.

Another important challenge is automating chemical plants. These facilities face an array of issues, including ballooning maintenance costs for aging equipment, shortages of maintenance personnel, and regulatory compliance at both the local and global levels. The plants contain vast numbers of pipes and specialized equipment that demand considerable effort to inspect and ensure proper maintenance. There is a growing need to automate plant maintenance operations with sensors that monitor equipment status in real time. We expect IOWN will offer solutions to this challenge. Along with monitoring equipment, maintenance will entail the use of drones and robots. Further into the future, we can imagine the scope expanding to data management across all areas of the chemical plant industry, including supply chains.

Other conceivable use cases include managing network equipment such as utility poles and underground/undersea cables, healthcare management for predicting major outbreaks of infectious diseases, smart grid management to predict and control power supply and demand in next-generation power grids, and society management to achieve sustainability by simulating a society and guiding its individuals and government toward optimal behavior.

The IOWN Global Forum's Vision for the Future

As this chapter has shown, the IOWN Global Forum brings together companies with diverse perspectives from a wide range of sectors. Together, we are working hard on numerous projects, from writing specifications to developing use cases. Let us reiterate that the progress thus far greatly exceeds our initial expectations and stands as a testament to the growing global excitement about the IOWN Initiative.

What lies ahead for the IOWN Global Forum? As a member of this body, let us introduce the future to which we aspire.

As a very young organization that has existed for just a little over four years, it is crucial that we remain focused on recruiting new members while making sure those who joined us from an early point are increasingly satisfied with their membership.

Promptly starting up businesses is more persuasive

We believe the key will be our approach to adding an increasing number of promising use cases. The best way to win people over is to demonstrate IOWN's effectiveness by showing how we can use it to solve real-world problems. APN IOWN 1.0 launched in 2023 as a commercial service, and IOWN 2.0 is coming in 2025. It seems that the most important thing right now is to start up businesses in different sectors and add more use cases.

However, because IOWN has implications for such a broad range of fields, the IOWN Global Forum alone cannot cover everything. Therefore, rather than deciding all matters on our own, we are thinking about working with organizations in closely related domains such as: the Linux Foundation, a non-profit organization working on major innovations through open source software; OpenROADM, which is writing open specifications to interconnect functions in optical transmission network devices; the Telecom Infra Project (TIP), an NPO established under Meta's leadership to transform telecommunications infrastructure; and the Optical Internetworking Forum (OIF), an industry organization for optical network technology.

To create the future we aspire to with IOWN, we need support from many partners. They include companies developing technology, as well as those that will use IOWN to address the issues their industries and society face. Both hold great importance to accomplishing our goals. We hope to elicit interest from as many companies, organizations, and groups as possible in the IOWN Global Forum so that we can shape the future together.

Key People Speak on the IOWN Global Forum

For a Sustainable Future

Rong-Shy Lin,
President, Chunghwa Telecom

As President of Chunghwa Telecom, a Taiwanese telecommunications company, Lin oversees a range of areas such as 5G, AI, big data, and cloud computing. He promotes enterprise digital transformation (DX), the integration of information and communications technologies, and the fostering of an agile corporate culture.
(Photo courtesy of Chunghwa Telecom)

● Reducing environmental impact while sustaining growth

Chunghwa Telecom joined the IOWN Global Forum early on, in April 2020. We are the largest integrated telecommunications company in Taiwan, aiming to provide high-quality and innovative ICT services. With an eye towards the next communication and computing infrastructure, current telecommunication networks still have room for enhancements in areas such as bandwidth and delay, mainly due to the conversion of optical and electrical signals and delays in network equipment. In addition, big data processing, cloud computing, and AI are driving a rapid increase in demand for data center resources, making energy efficiency a global challenge.

One of our visions is to become an international benchmark enterprise built upon sustainable development. To achieve this, we need next-generation communications and computing technologies. We believe that the technologies proposed by the IOWN Global Forum, such as the APN (All-Photonic Network) and DCI (Data-Centric Infrastructure), which realize low power consumption, ultra-wideband, and ultra-low delay, will greatly contribute to the sustainable growth of Chunghwa Telecom, and reduce environmental impact.

To realize the vision of the IOWN Global Forum, there are still many issues to be resolved, such as technical verification, standardization, and the development of technical specifications. To address these issues, experts from various fields participating in the forum need to cooperate, promote joint research and discussion, and develop ICT technologies and application services in an integrated manner.

● Taking on the challenge of innovation with our brand spirit

We at Chunghwa Telecom actively participate in the IOWN Global Forum in various fields, in line with our brand spirit of " Always Ahead ." For example, in October 2023, we signed an MoU with our good friends at NTT to realize international network connectivity and announced a demonstration experiment that aimed to connect Japan and Taiwan using IOWN APN and DCI technologies.

We are also working on the development of immersive video experiences using volumetric video that reconstructs three-dimensional space from captured images. By engaging in these technical demonstrations, we intend to push the boundaries of the technology and accelerate the development and implementation of IOWN technologies.

● For ourselves and future generations

We participate in the IOWN Global Forum to create innovative technologies. That is why we invite software and hardware suppliers, service providers, academic institutions, and research institutes join the IOWN Global Forum, and work together to make our visions a reality.

Due to rapid technological advancements, smarter, more sustainable, and more efficient communications infrastructure has become essential in many industries. The IOWN Global Forum plays an important role in making this happen. We cannot achieve this goal without the participation of various sectors, including technology, telecommunications, and electronics.

We wish to create a smart world through innovations that transform communication and information exchange. This is a noble vision, which is why we need the participation of our partners who share it. Together, I believe we can create a better world for ourselves and future generations by building an intelligent and secure communications and computing infrastructure we can be proud of.

Key People Speak on the IOWN Global Forum

Looking Forward to Strong Leadership

Gilles Bourdon,
Vice President of Wireline Networks & Infrastructure, Orange Innovation

As Vice President of Wireline Networks & Infrastructure at Orange Innovation, a French telecommunications company Orange, Bourdon oversees various fields from fiber optic networks to home networks such as wireless LANs, and routers. He also promotes innovation throughout the group.
(Photo courtesy of Orange Innovation)

● The first European telecommunications carriers to join

Orange was the first European telecom company to join the IOWN Global Forum as a sponsor shortly after its establishment. We have had a strong interest in IOWN since the beginning as we have formed various partnerships with NTT. When I heard about the IOWN Global Forum, I was convinced that the direction of IOWN aligned with Orange's vision.

It was important that we participate as a European company to bring a European perspective to the IOWN Global Forum. Looking back now, I wish we had joined earlier.

● Breakthroughs are needed to achieve our vision

We aim to achieve higher performance and higher energy efficiency through the activities of the IOWN Global Forum. To achieve this, we need technological breakthroughs that exceed the pace of technological evolution to date, and we need to work toward common goals across the industry.

As a breakthrough technology, we aim to build an optical network called an APN. Although optical transmission technology has been around for a long time, conventional optical transmission has low operational flexibility. APNs enable more flexible interoperable optical networks.

The IOWN Global Forum has defined many use cases, and they all require light to achieve them. I think the entire communications industry, including equipment manufacturers, needs to promote APN.

● First, promote digital twin networks

We're working on various APN architectures and use cases, and one of the first examples we're looking at is a digital twin of the network. I mentioned earlier that existing optical networks are not flexible because there are a lot of hidden variables in the network and coordination is very complex. If we take all the variables from the actual network and reconstruct them on a digital twin, we can simulate various situations and perform optimal operations.

There are many elements in a network such as fiber-optic users and cell phone base stations, etc. And every communication is converted from electricity to light and from light to electricity many times, consuming a lot of energy each time. Therefore, we're trying to make an optical connection as seamless possible from one end of the line to the other. Digital twins are an important step in achieving this.

● Leadership expected from telecommunications companies

I feel that NTT is strongly leading the IOWN Global Forum. Whenever I talk to Dr. Kawazoe (NTT Senior Executive Vice President), IOWN Global Forum President and Chairperson, I always feel the strength of his belief and vision for IOWN.

The IOWN Global Forum can be separated into three main sectors: users, equipment vendors, and operators. The equipment vendors in particular are very active and doing a great job. However, the network vision should be led by the telecom operators. In this sense, I expect NTT to continue to show strong leadership.

[Chapter 4]

The Future IOWN
Will Bring About

IOWN & AI

So far in this book, we have seen what IOWN is, where it stands at present, the direction of the technology's evolution, and how IOWN is winning support around the world. Chapter 4 will look ahead to introduce how IOWN will shape the future.

A starting point to addressing AI-related problems

First, let us consider a future where IOWN and AI work in tandem.

As you have seen several times already, society is consuming power at a rapidly increasing pace. One of the major factors behind this is the spread of AI. ChatGPT, released by OpenAI in November 2022, can generate text that is almost indistinguishable from that written by a human. It has fundamentally changed how we regard AI.

For example, if you give ChatGPT instructions with natural speech, as if directing an employee or asking a friend for a favor, it can immediately complete tasks such as writing sentences and taglines, summarizing long passages, translating, creating tables, or analyzing numerical data. Furthermore, it depends on the given task and how you write the prompt, but in many cases, the quality of the response is almost as good as a human's. ChatGPT became an overnight global success, mainly for business use, and in just two months gained over one hundred million users, an astonishing pace that set a record for an online service.

To catch up with ChatGPT, American big tech like Google and Meta have been improving their own generative AI solutions in an intensifying AI arms race. Meanwhile, a knock-on effect of this torrid pace of AI development is the sharp uptick in computation at data centers, as mentioned earlier in this book.

Generative AI tools like ChatGPT perform inference and other processes based on a large language model (LLM). Creating an LLM requires deep learning on massive quantities of text in numerous documents and books, and constructing the model involves a huge amount of computing power. We can express the size or scale of an LLM according to the number of parameters it contains. The GPT-3 model used in the first version of ChatGPT had 175 billion parameters. As mentioned in the Introduction, building GPT-3's LLM needed around 1,300 megawatt-hours[1] of electricity, which is more than the electricity generated in an hour by a 1,000-megawatt nuclear power plant. GPT-4, released in 2023, reportedly contains more than 1 trillion parameters, far more than GPT-3.

In July 2024, Meta announced Llama 3.1, which has up to 405 billion parameters. As you can see, the AI performance race is also a contest to see who can create the largest system. LLMs are already measured against each other in trillions of parameters rather than billions.

As other companies in addition to the big tech are also developing their own AIs, we can expect AI-related power consumption to continue its rapid expansion. However, the Earth does not have an inexhaustible supply of power, and it seems that at some point we will reach a limit. Even though renewable energy sources such as solar and wind power continue to grow, many countries still rely on fossil fuels. Therefore, consuming more power will directly lead to more carbon emissions.

To combat climate change, we must reduce our energy consumption as much as possible, but AI presents an obstacle. On the other hand, creating a sustainable society requires innovation, including advances in AI. Humanity thus faces seemingly irreconcilable issues surrounding the fast-evolving technology of AI.

Again, IOWN is a starting point to addressing these AI-related conundrums. One ultimate goal with IOWN is to achieve one hundred times greater power efficiency in ICT equipment using photonics-electronics convergence devices. Simply put, this would enable AI with equivalent performance to today's tools to run on one hundredth the power.

In addition to reducing power consumption, we believe that IOWN will become a critical piece of the foundation facilitating AI's evolution. The next sections will present specific examples of the world we envision with IOWN and AI.

NTT's proprietary LLM: tsuzumi

Let's start with the AI that NTT is developing. We have built tsuzumi, an LLM to serve as the foundation for generative AI. Commercial service launched in March 2024. tsuzumi's four distinguishing features are that it is lightweight, excellent at handling Japanese, flexibly customizable, and multimodal.

tsuzumi comes in two lightweight versions: the Lightweight Version with seven billion parameters and the Ultra-Lightweight Version with six hundred million parameters. Compared to the big LLMs like GPT-3 mentioned above, the Lightweight Version is about one twenty-fifth the size, while the Ultra-Lightweight Version is approximately one three-hundredths the size. These smaller sizes allow the user to cut down on power usage and training costs. After an LLM is built, it must perform calculations called "inference" whenever it is used. tsuzumi can also significantly reduce the inference cost compared to GPT-3, with the Lightweight Version being roughly twenty times more efficient and the Ultra-Lightweight Version around seventy times more.

One might think that fewer parameters must mean lower performance, but it is not so simple. This point is related to the different direction we are aiming for with our AI.

If ChatGPT and other AIs are gigantic know-it-all models enlarged through the amount of training their LLMs have undergone, tsuzumi is a small model with specialized knowledge. By training an LLM with a focus on specific industries and areas of expertise, we can expect quality responses with only a relatively small amount of training. Our intention with tsuzumi is for it to specialize in certain fields, rather than being a generalist that can handle any topic.

Performance also varies according to the data used for training. ChatGPT, which was developed in the United States, is trained on English-centric data that includes only a small amount of Japanese data. In contrast, tsuzumi, which was created in Japan, was designed with Japanese training data that is better both qualitatively and quantitatively to process the Japanese language at a high level.

Including these aspects, tsuzumi's second distinctive feature is that it excels at handling the Japanese language. Research into natural language processing (NLP) is key to developing LLMs. This is a field we have spent over forty years studying at NTT. In 2022, NTT ranked twelfth in the world and first in Japan for the number of AI-related papers published.[2] We are also a world leader in Japanese NLP, having received more awards for excellence from the Association for Natural Language Processing (ANLP) than any other corporate research institute over the past decade.

By applying the results of many years of NLP research, tsuzumi has shown that it performs well in various benchmark tests, especially when processing Japanese.

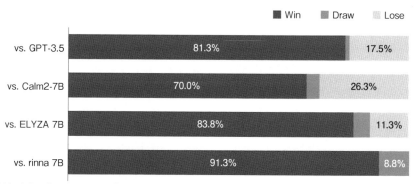

Figure 4-1 – Japanese Language Performance Comparison of NTT LLM tsuzumi with Rakuda benchmark

*Rakuda benchmark: executed October 22, 2023
Graded on forty questions about Japanese geography, politics, history, and society, evaluated through a comparison of two models by GPT-4 (40 questions x 2 presentation orders)
The model outputs used were those uploaded to the site, except for LLM-jp, which followed the configuration entered on the Hugging Face model card.
Input repetitions and terminal tokens excluded in post processing.
Assessment scores produced through comparison conducted by GPT-4 between tsuzumi-7b and each model listed on the leaderboard as of September 27, 2023. Results ranked according to Bradley-Terry strengths.

Figure 4-1 shows the results of a performance comparison using Rakuda, a generative AI benchmark. Rakuda uses GPT-4 to assess the output of two LLMs according to their general ability to process the Japanese language, including sentence structure and fluency. The results of comparisons between the Lightweight Version of tsuzumi and other AIs show that the former leads in terms of Japanese language performance, beating GPT-3.5 more than 80 percent of the time and the CyberAgent Calm2-7b LLM for Japanese more than 70 percent of the time.

The third distinctive feature is flexible customizability. By combining a pre-trained LLM with a small "adapter" model with additional training, tsuzumi can add industry-specific knowledge and expressions.

One example of what this lets you do is perform precise, yet low-cost customization tailored to specific operations by preparing adapters for different users and situations, such as an industry-specific adapter trained with that industry's typical terminology and knowledge, or a company/organization-specific adapter trained with the business processes and rules of that particular organization (Figure 4-2).

There is also a multi-adapter feature that can toggle or combine adapters on top of the base model, depending on how you want to use it. This capability can enable greater accuracy from the synergies gained from switching and mixing adapters for sales, R&D, marketing, or the like.

With a boost to performance from customizing specific tasks, tsuzumi achieved Japanese language performance in these tasks that, compared to the initial releases of GPT-3.5 and GPT-4, was better by approximately 70 percent and 50 percent, respectively.

Figure 4-2 – Tuning Enabled by tsuzumi

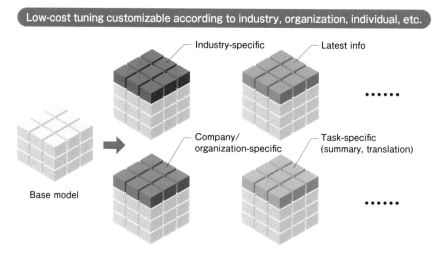

tsuzumi's fourth intriguing feature is its multimodal functionality. This allows tsuzumi to handle multiple types of data in addition to language, such as visual and audio data. At present, tsuzumi can understand combinations of language and visual or audio data, allowing it to read and provide answers about graphs, diagrams, and other images.

For example, imagine that you show tsuzumi a chart showing the NTT Group's greenhouse gas emissions over time and ask, "By what percentage will IOWN reduce power consumption by 2040?" It will respond with an answer like "−45%" (Figure 4-3).

We are also pursuing research on combining language with physicality. Specifically, we are studying how to give tsuzumi a sense of physicality by installing it into a robot. In a demonstration we designed, a robot was given

Chapter 4 – The Future IOWN Will Bring About

Figure 4-3 – tsuzumi Answer on Reduced Power Consumption from IOWN by 2040, Based on GHG Emissions Chart

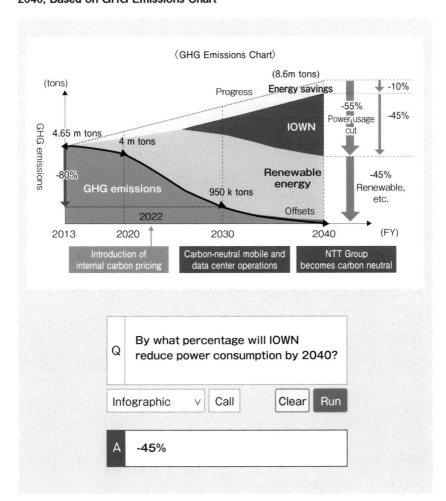

the following instructions: "Set the dinner table with a meal that would warm the diner on a cold winter's day. Remember to set the table for a left-handed person." The tsuzumi robot analyzed the instructions, took into account nutritional balance and seasonal factors, and designed a meal with the main dish being a curry that would warm the body, with sides of salad and spring rolls. The robot served each dish while explaining why it was chosen. It also placed the chopsticks and spoons in a way that was easy for a left-handed person to use.

AI needs diversity, too

By specializing in the Japanese language and enabling customization, we have made tsuzumi into a model that is lightweight and highly effective in specific fields. We believe that this approach of combining lightweight models will be important in developing the AIs of the future.

One reason is that it's easier to improve performance this way. There is also research showing that, compared to developing one gigantic model, it's easier to improve performance by merging multiple lightweight models into a new LLM.[3]

Of even greater importance is ensuring diversity. We can imbue AI with diversity by combining specialized lightweight AIs. As explained in Chapter 1, LLMs are created by training them on vast amounts of existing data and statistically deriving the best answer. However, if a single giant AI that has been trained on the world's data gives an answer, could you refute it? If that answer is wrong, would anyone notice?

Humanity is trying to create the best society for everyone by recognizing diversity and taking each other's perspectives into account when discussing matters. Likewise, if AI continues to evolve and becomes more integrated into our lives, AI must be designed with diversity, rather than being an absolute entity. Diverse AIs with their own traits and areas of expertise will collaborate and cooperate with each other, reaching answers through discussions from different perspectives. This is the preferred approach to addressing social issues through the power of AI.

Our vision, therefore, is not one gigantic, all-knowing AI, but rather a constellation of diverse, smaller AIs with their own specialties and personalities, working together and cooperating to address society's problems with their collective intelligence. We call this concept an "AI constellation." This is, so to speak, the democratization of AI, where the democratic processes of modern society are applied to AI (Figure 4-4). And as the

Figure 4-4 – NTT's AI Vision: AI Constellations

- Solve social issues through the collective intelligence of small LLMs with expertise and personalities, rather than one giant LLM with knowledge of everything.
- IOWN will be important as the foundation for collaboration between numerous LLMs.

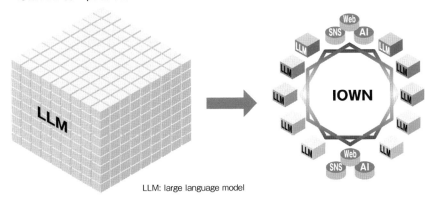

LLM: large language model

foundation for collaboration between masses of AIs, IOWN will play a major role.

AI constellations will reveal lines of reasoning

Another advantage of an AI constellation is that processes are easier to see. If you leave everything to a single large AI, it is harder to see how it arrived at an answer. The AI's reasoning between your prompt and the response it comes to is a black box. Even developers find it difficult to explain why an AI arrives at the answers it provides.

OpenAI recently broke down GPT-4's reasoning into sixteen million interpretable patterns,[4] but such research on AI's logic is still in its infancy. This means that even if there are biases or errors in the AI's rationale, it is still difficult to evaluate and correct them. Also, because today's AI uses sentences written by humans and is designed so that humans teach it the "correct answers," it is impossible to eliminate our social biases pertaining to race, culture, and gender. Some say that an AI can also be heavily influenced by its designers' way of thinking.

However, if you use a system that integrates multiple AIs, you can have AIs with diverse backgrounds discuss and make decisions from their different perspectives. This approach also allows you to see the interactions between the AIs. Of course, AIs will converse with each other much faster than humans do, perhaps exchanging thousands or tens of thousands of messages in an instant. But when you later review the process step by step, you can check the discussion that led to the final answer. Therefore, even if the conclusion is questionable, we can validate it by checking the discussion's progression for any irregularities, and if there are any, make corrections and redo the conversation. This approach can improve the conclusion's accuracy and persuasiveness.

In November 2023, NTT concluded an agreement to collaborate with AI startup Sakana AI on developing AI constellations.[5] The Tokyo-based company was established by two of the world's leading AI experts: David Ha, who led Google's AI research in Japan, and Llion Jones, one of the authors of the famous paper proposing the "transformer model" that became the basis for today's generative AI. NTT and Sakana AI have teamed up because they share a vision of AI constellations with small, diverse AIs work together.

Sakana AI found inspiration from the evolutionary process in the natural world to develop advanced AI. Their innovative approach involves the creation of groups of small AIs that work together like a school of fish. NTT brings to the partnership more than forty years of research into NLP and our cutting-edge IOWN technology.

By combining our technologies and skills, we seek to develop AI constellations that will enable more efficient collaboration while reducing the problematic consumption of large amounts of power by current large AI models. Through this joint research, we are striving to create a sustainable AI society that not only has a lower environmental impact by consuming less power, but also generates new knowledge and value to solve complex social issues.

Efficient collaboration between multiple AIs

We have covered AI at length. Now let us address the age-old issue of how to correctly synchronize a large distributed system like an AI constellation. When running a large number of interconnected AIs at high speed, it is vital that any wasted communication be eliminated by ensuring that each system sends signals at exactly the right time. With the conventional internet, however, factors such as the state of the connection make such precise synchronization impossible, which presents difficulties in very precisely and efficiently coordinating the timing of interactions. This is where IOWN's advantages come into play, as it is based on optical technology enabling fast communication that is incredibly stable, while also offering features such as accurate synchronization.

If you group ten people in a room for a conversation, they will have no problems with latency. But when holding a remote meeting with all the participants located far away from each other and communicating over poor connections, people end up speaking over each other and smooth discussion becomes difficult. The same thing can happen in collaboration between AIs.

Using IOWN, which enables stable, fast, precise transmissions, will allow a large number of AIs to communicate with great speed and precision, as if they were all in the same room. For this reason, IOWN will be an indispensable technology serving as the communications infrastructure for AI constellations.

Let's consider some specific examples of social issues that AI constellations may be able to solve (Figure 4-5).

Figure 4-5 – AI Constellation Concept to Realize General-Purpose AI

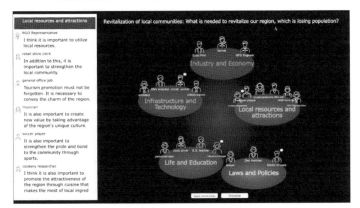

Imagine that several AIs with different areas of expertise are having a conversation. One represents an NGO, while the others are a store clerk, a clerical worker, a musician, a soccer player, and a culinary expert. The topic is about solving local issues, with each AI answering the question, "What do we need to do to stimulate the local economy amid a declining population?"

……

NGO Representative AI: I think it is important to utilize local resources.

retail store clerk AI: In addition to this, it is important to strengthen the local community.

general office job AI: Tourism promotion must not be forgotten. It is necessary to convey the charm of the region.

musician AI: It is also important to create new value by taking advantage of the region's unique culture.

soccer player AI: It is also important to strengthen the pride and bond to the community through sports.

cookery researcher AI: I think it is also important to promote the attractiveness of the region through cuisine that makes the most of local ingred...

This is how AIs will bring their different perspectives to a conversation and find common ground between each other so as to form a consensus on how to address a complex problem with multiple solutions. They will then discuss and refine their ideas to find solutions to a problem that humans would have trouble even defining.

To take the concept a step further, we could arrange ten thousand AIs with profiles similar to the population of a municipality and place them in large simulations. A discussion between this many humans would be impossible, but ten thousand AIs might wrap it up in a moment. Traditional democracy is indirect in that decisions are made by elected representatives. However, utilizing AI constellations could allow us to create a new form of democracy in which the policy discussions reflect the voices of residents on a more granular level.

Four use cases for AI constellations

We see four areas for AI constellation use cases.

One is large social simulations, such as the huge discussion among local residents and analysis of public opinion described above. In addition to politics, the technology could simulate marketing and social media commentary. In fields of academic research such as sociology and psychology, AI simulations could be employed alongside conventional observational research.

Second is large project management, such as for a major software development project, corporate management, or managing a neighborhood association. Using AI constellations would allow for a multifaceted perspective on complex issues and enable the incorporation of ideas that an individual or small team would not have thought of on their own.

Third is AI refinement and AI governance to improve upon AI's reliability, ethics, and diversity. With multiple AIs working together, they could monitor each other from their different perspectives. This would help reduce AI "hallucinations" that generate information unsupported by facts, as well as introduce diverse opinions to reduce bias.

The fourth use case is digital twin of people. AI would create these digital replicas in a virtual space. By linking your AI-generated avatar with another person's, you could perform various simulations. For example, you could delegate some of your work to your avatar and give yourself time to interact with more people. You could also simulate sales and customer support, or even romantic relationships in your personal life. You could also create digital duplicates of experts and celebrities whom you could ask to give lectures or offer advice.

We believe that AI constellations, which link numerous lightweight AIs and harness their collective intelligence to solve problems, will become extremely important to shaping the direction of AI development. And IOWN will be essential as the basis for this process.

IOWN & Quantum Computers

Next, let's look at the future that IOWN and quantum computers will usher in.

Quantum computers hold promise for bringing about a data-driven society. Whereas current computers perform calculations using bits represented by zeroes and ones, the quantum bits, or qubits, at the heart of quantum computing can exist in a state of superposition, in which they are both zeroes and ones. This will enable quantum computers to instantly perform enormous calculations that would take a conventional computer tens of thousands of years.

Practical quantum computers are probably still a long way off, but there are many common threads between this technology and IOWN.

We have drawn up the IOWN roadmap from 1.0 to 4.0. IOWN 1.0 is the All-Photonics Network (APN) that employs light along all network routes, IOWN 2.0 is about connecting boards, IOWN 3.0 is for connecting chips with light, and IOWN 4.0 concerns optical connections inside chips. In the roadmap, 1.0 covers networks, while 2.0 and beyond deal with computing, but every one of these is about connecting objects with light. In a future with IOWN and quantum computers, we will finally see the use of optical technology in the actual computations.

Quantum computing, the ultimate goal of IOWN

Development is proceeding on several different design approaches to quantum computing. They include the superconducting method, using silicon, and the optical approach. NTT is researching how to create an optical design.

What makes the optical method different from the superconducting and silicon-based approaches is that it uses light for quantum computation instead of electrons. The most important element of an optical design is the quantum light source that generates the optical pulses used for quantum bits and calculations. This is where we can apply IOWN technology. The roadmap released thus far goes up to IOWN 4.0, but beyond that, IOWN 5.0 and 6.0 may include computations with light and optical quantum computers.

Another advantage to the optical approach is that optical quantum computers could process quickly at room temperature, unlike electron-based designs that require cooling to extremely low temperatures. An optical quantum computer has no need for a large cooling system, which makes it easy to scale up and allows it to run while consuming little power. We should note that research on optical quantum computers is still in the early stages and their performance, in terms of how many qubits they can handle, is still far behind superconducting quantum computers and other designs. However, rapid progress is underway, and if the trend continues, optical quantum computers could at some point overtake other designs.

An optical quantum computer would use light for communication and reduce power consumption. Not only that, but using light would make

121

computation itself yet more efficient. When one thinks about it this way, quantum computers may very well be the ultimate goal for IOWN.

Regardless of the design one uses, connecting quantum computers to each other requires a quantum network that can immediately transmit large amounts of data and maintain robust security. That network must also be able to transmit data in quantum states without converting it to electricity and it must be connected with light. That means that the IOWN infrastructure for quantum communications has to be in place before we can usher in the quantum age.

People hold different opinions on when quantum computers will become a practical reality, but the mainstream view is sometime around 2050, so it's still a long way off. The advent of generative AI, however, has led to rapid advances in artificial intelligence. Likewise, it is entirely possible that quantum computing will experience unexpected technological innovations, bringing about the quantum age sooner than expected.

IOWN in the Wider Society

So far, we have focused on computing to examine how IOWN may shape our world in the near future. In networks, meanwhile, commercial All-Photonics Network (APN) services have already launched. The ultra-high speed and ultra-low latency in APNs also have the potential to change all kinds of industries in the not-too-distant future. We will now consider what the future holds for IOWN in the network domain by examining possible applications in different industries and fields.

Construction: remotely operated construction machinery to address labor shortages

At construction sites in Japan, issues such as a shortage of labor, long working hours, and increasingly older engineers are growing more serious. As the country's population is expected to continue shrinking and graying, addressing these problems is an urgent matter. One promising solution is remotely operated construction machinery, which require specialized skills to operate.[6]

In fact, some construction sites are using this equipment to ensure safety. However, there is still significant latency between the operator's actions and the resulting movement. This, along with matters such as safety concerns, limit the extent to which builders can use remotely operated construction machinery. For example, boring and transporting rock out of the end of a narrow tunnel can be dangerous and highly technical work. Remote systems are already in development, but the operator must be within a few hundred meters. This makes it difficult to install a cockpit outside the tunnel.

Installing an IOWN APN in a harsh environment like this could allow operators to remotely control construction machinery from a safe location dozens or hundreds of kilometers away.

Tower cranes erected on buildings under construction are another type of construction machinery that needs remote operation. An operator of this equipment must have advanced specialist skills. First, one must climb a long ladder to the operator's seat high up in the air. Once there, the operator has to remain for many hours until the work is finished. The work environment is extremely demanding, as the shaking from strong winds or earthquakes can be terrifying. Meanwhile, tower crane operators are in short supply.

IOWN will make work at construction sites much safer. It will also deliver a major contribution to the addressing of social issues such as labor shortages and long working hours, in part by facilitating training for new operators.

NTT is already conducting Proof-of-Concept tests on remote operation in collaboration with construction industry partners. For example, we connected a remote operation system jointly developed by Komatsu and its subsidiary EARTHBRAIN with an IOWN APN. Linked via an APN from Tokyo, we demonstrated remote control of a hydraulic excavator in Chiba Prefecture (Figure 4-6). By transmitting high-resolution 4K footage of the construction site with no degradation and low latency, the operator could accurately monitor the situation and control the machinery smoothly from a remote location.

We are also working on remote operation of tower cranes. In collaboration with Takenaka Corporation, we conducted a demonstration for remote operation of a tower crane installed at the company's West Japan Equipment Center in Sakai, Osaka Prefecture, via an APN from Tokyo. To ensure the quality of work that skilled remote operators can perform, Takenaka has set an acceptable latency limit of five hundred milliseconds. This test confirmed the feasibility of remote operation with an acceptable latency over the five hundred kilometers between Tokyo and Osaka via the APN.

Applying this sort of remote operation to more construction machinery will

Figure 4-6 – Remote Operation System Developed by Komatsu and EARTHBRAIN

mean fewer workers are required at sites, leading to less overtime and easier hiring challenges.

Medicine: telehealth to correct regional disparities in care

In medical care, telesurgery is one promising use case for IOWN. There are fewer aspiring surgeons in Japan these days. The shortage of surgeons is particularly acute in rural areas. If surgery could be performed remotely from a distant location, there would be a lower burden on both physicians and patients, such as the need to travel, and patients in rural areas could receive the same level of care as those in cities.

Remotely operated robotic-assisted surgical systems are already in use for some operations. This is because a robot can perform precise movements more accurately and steadily than a human hand. However, remote operation comes with challenges in terms of communication line latency and stability, so these robots are usually controlled from an adjacent room.

Surgeons say that when they perform an operation, it's not the amount of latency that poses so much of a problem, but rather irregular fluctuations in that latency. If a robot's movements occur with a consistently slight delay relative to the surgeon's movements, the surgeon can anticipate and perform the operation accordingly. However, if latency is inconsistent, with the robot responding immediately at certain times and more slowly at others, performing the operation becomes difficult. An APN experiences little latency and no fluctuations, even over long distances, thereby enabling telesurgery from entirely different regions.

In November 2022, we demonstrated telesurgery with Japanese robotic-assisted surgery system developer Medicaroid. By connecting the company's hinotori Surgical Robot System to an APN, we sought to create a "shared space," so to speak, where physically separated environments were combined into one allowing for smooth surgery.[7]

NTT's Musashino Research and Development Center in Musashino, Tokyo hosted a testing environment for an APN providing a link to a robotic-assisted surgical system about one hundred kilometers away. The test confirmed the feasibility of remotely operating a surgical robot just like when performing surgery in person, as there was very nearly zero fluctuation in latency. Furthermore, the test proved the feasibility of sharing information on the entire spatial environment, including 8K ultra-high-definition video and audio, to create a shared surgical environment that is just like performing surgery in the same space. We will continue this research to encourage more telesurgery with APNs.

We conducted another test in March 2022, this one to demonstrate a cloud endoscopy system with Olympus.[8] Modern endoscopes have advanced assistive features that process high-definition images captured by the endoscope's camera to alert the operator to areas that may be diseased. However, since all of these advanced features process the data in the endoscope, it is difficult to boost performance or to perform updates or other maintenance.

This is why NTT and Olympus are working on cloud endoscopy to distribute some of the more demanding tasks, such as image processing, to the cloud. The endoscope connects to a data center via an APN. The device sends its camera footage via a low-latency transmission to the data center, where it is processed and sent back to the endoscope over the same network and displayed on a monitor. This arrangement enables heavy image processing that the endoscope would struggle to handle on its own. It also allows software updates to install the latest features on the cloud. Another benefit is that hospitals could share imagery to remotely provide diagnoses and care in real time.

In medicine, the use of APNs to facilitate telehealth is helping to address social issues such as medical staff shortages and disparities in access to care.

Broadcasting: remote production to enhance live broadcasts

IOWN will also help address issues in the broadcasting industry. One example is remote production that will change how live programs are created.

127

When broadcasting a concert, or a live sporting event like a baseball game or soccer match, a production truck usually has to be at the venue. Since the line transmitting video to the broadcasting station has limited capacity, the truck has to first receive footage from multiple cameras at the venue, produce video from that footage, then transmit the edited data to the broadcasting station.

Using a high-speed, high-capacity APN, however, would allow the broadcaster to send all the camera footage in real time to the station, where the staff can produce the program while switching between camera views. This would streamline the process of deploying equipment and personnel to the stadium or other venue when dispatching a production truck. It would also allow the broadcasting station to use more advanced editing equipment. The result would be a program with more camera angles and other added value.

The NTT Group tested this remote production approach in July 2023 with the J.League, Japan's professional soccer league, at the Meiji Yasuda J.League World Challenge 2023 Powered by Docomo, an event at the National Stadium in Tokyo.[9] The stadium and eXeField Akiba, an esports facility in Tokyo's Akihabara district, were connected via an APN to transmit footage from multiple broadcast cameras. Switching cameras and other production work happened at eXeField. The high-quality edited data was then transmitted to a broadcasting station.

High-speed, low-latency video transmission is a technology that could also serve as the basis for creating new entertainment experiences, such as virtual reality and interactive viewing. We can expect even more such applications for IOWN in the future.

Data backup: distributing backups in real time

Many companies prepare for emergencies by storing backup data in locations spread out across different regions. That way, even if a major disaster hits one area, the company won't lose access to the data it needs for business continuity. Data security is especially important in the financial sector, which handles data on transactions involving large sums of money, but the bigger issue here is backup frequency. Current networks aren't fast enough to transfer the enormous amount of transaction data, but even if they had the same speed and capacity as an APN, the difference in the networks' effective transfer speed can be up to 1.7 times.[10] This is because protocols such as TCP/IP are sensitive to latency. For this reason, increasing backup frequency is impossible with existing networks.

For example, if a company backs up data only once a day, a disaster could wipe out a day's worth of transaction data. However, data centers in different locations connected via high-speed, high-capacity APNs could back up trading data nearly in real time and store it in multiple locations. This would effectively eliminate the risk of losing data in a disaster.10 In the future, this sort of backup capability should be in high demand.

Backed up data also requires maintenance considerations. Many companies use data centers in downtown areas for backups because they can quickly dispatch personnel in the event of an equipment failure or other problem. In the future, the NTT Group is considering using IOWN to remotely operate maintenance robots at far-away data centers.

Esports: creating fair online competitions free from latency's impact

The type of entertainment where low latency is the most important could be esports. Timing is of vital importance in esports competitions, where tenths or even hundredths of a second matter. The slightest delay in relaying a player's input can spell the difference between victory and defeat. One particular issue is latency in the lines connecting esports gaming devices. If latency varies from player to player, the competition cannot be fair.

This problem has posed difficulties in holding top-level esports tournaments online, so it has been standard practice to hold them in one location to avoid giving any player a competitive edge arising from network conditions. At the tournaments that are held online, many players have elected not to join due to the inconsistent gaming environment.

However, using an APN with consistently low latency would enable a gaming environment with equal conditions for all players. For example, each player could receive a precisely determined handicap according to their latency. The highest level of esports events could also happen online, something that has been difficult with the conventional internet. Furthermore, connecting competition and spectator venues with an APN would allow fans watching in other parts of the country or beyond to join in cheering on the players along with the crowd at the venue, without any noticeable delay.

To verify IOWN's effectiveness in esports, the NTT Group used an APN to organize a demonstration in March 2023. The full name of the event was: Open New Gate for Esports 2023-The Future of Esports Created by

IOWN.[11] Two Tokyo locations, Shibuya and Akihabara, hosted the event. The PCs running the games were in Akihabara, while Shibuya hosted the gaming displays, headsets, keyboards, and mice. The APN connected these peripherals to the PCs in Akihabara.

The demonstration showed that professional esports competitors could play the games while in Shibuya without experiencing any latency issues. Looking ahead, we believe that holding esports tournaments by connecting different locations will also help stimulate local economies.

Smart cities: an information distribution platform for big data

Efforts to bring IOWN to urban planning are also underway. In the future, cyber-physical systems (CPS), designed for optimization by acquiring and processing detailed data from the real world, will likely become widespread. As the amount of information collected from urban infrastructure and IoT devices explodes, IOWN will play a key role as an information distribution platform for real-time transmission and processing of this big data.

In June 2023, the NTT Group announced an agreement with Tokyu Land Corporation to collaborate on new urban development projects by leveraging technologies and services associated with the IOWN Initiative.[12] Facilities that Tokyu Land is involved with in Greater Shibuya, which covers a 2.5-kilometer radius from Shibuya Station in Tokyo, will be the model area for introducing IOWN services. One example is an idea to connect offices via APN to project each one's conference rooms on large high-resolution displays, enabling meetings that feel like an in-person discussion. Another idea is to place robots and devices in shopping complexes to provide cordial customer service from a remote location.

Incidentally, Shibuya Ward is the only local government, as of September 2024, to have joined the IOWN Global Forum, and is actively using IOWN in new urban development. The Shibuya area looks set to become a pilot model district for utilizing IOWN.

NTT Group company NTT Urban Solutions is also engaged in urban development with IOWN through its work on urban Digital Twin Computing (DTC). The work involves using data on the city and its citizens. This data comes from sensors installed around town and in smartphones and other personal devices. The data undergoes predictive analysis in a virtual space called a "digital twin." The results are then fed back to the real world. In the future, Mobility as a Service (MaaS) solutions that optimize travel through a combination of different modes of transport, as well as logistics optimization solutions, will need IOWN-based data processing.

Space communications: a new future for space exploration with light data relays and HAPS

IOWN optical communications technology also has applications in space. One is optical data relay services. Observation satellites and other devices can collect enormous amounts of data in space, including high-resolution images of the Earth. However, one issue is how to transmit these satellites' data to the ground.

Consider low-orbit observation satellites. Since they orbit the Earth every 90 to 120 minutes, they can only communicate with facilities on the ground at certain times. Transmissions sent on radio waves also come with capacity limitations. Therefore, relaying the observation satellite data to a geostationary satellite in a higher orbit, then forwarding the data to a site on the ground via an optical data transmission, should allow for the transmission of large amounts of data nearly in real time.

This optical data relay technology will facilitate data collection from space and dramatically improve the accuracy of satellite sensing, leading to technological innovation in a wide range of fields, including weather forecasting, disaster prediction, agriculture, and security.

Looking further ahead, we are also working on space-based data centers. A combination of dozens or even hundreds of satellites in communication with each other will provide the same level of computing power as a data center. We could utilize the capabilities of such a data center in space to process the immense amounts of data from observation satellites and then send only the results to Earth, allowing us to more efficiently obtain incredibly accurate information.

Furthermore, since satellites run on solar energy, the limited power places constraints on an individual satellite's computing capability. In the future, though, satellites equipped with photonics-electronics convergence devices, which will be introduced with IOWN 2.0 and later, should have far better energy efficiency, thus expanding the range of applications for space-based computing yet further.

NTT launched a space business brand, NTT C89, in June 2024 (Figure 4-7).[13] In addition to the space data center business, NTT is vigorously pushing ahead with space-related businesses based on optical technology. They include a radio access network (RAN) business in space, which

Figure 4-7 – NTT President Akira Shimada Announcing Space Business Brand NTT C89 (June 2024)

employs a combination of regular satellites and high-altitude pseudo-satellites (HAPS) that fly automatically in the stratosphere, to expand cellular coverage to mountainous areas, the sea, and outer space. Another is a satellite phone business.

[Chapter 5]

Data Security and IOWN

Safeguarding the State's Data

As we have seen, the IOWN network can send quality transmissions with large amounts of data at high speed and with no latency. Furthermore, because it provides a dedicated line for each user, it can ensure a high level of security when sending data. We can expect such a network to handle data with the utmost care. Let us now consider the role that data plays in society.

This chapter will consider the significance data holds for organizations such as national governments and companies, as well as individuals, and introduce IOWN technology's role in safeguarding data.

The state is the data which defines it

Sadly, we still see wars and conflicts erupting in different places across the globe. There are also many countries in tense relations and diplomatic standoffs. Terrorist groups are trying to destabilize states and overthrow governments. Recent examples of ongoing conflicts include the Russo Ukrainian War and the fighting in the Gaza Strip. In such uncertain times, the state must always consider how to defend its land and citizens.

If a country comes under attack and the state has to mount a defensive effort for its land, where should it prioritize that defense? At the top of the list, of course, are the lives and property of citizens. And to keep the socioeconomic activity that sustains citizens running, the state must also maintain infrastructure services for roads, bridges, power plants, and so on.

However, with advances in digitalization, we cannot overlook the fact that socioeconomic activities and infrastructure services can only function with the data underlying them. In other words, in this era when we manage everything with digital data, it is crucial that we safeguard the data which defines the state.

For example, if one country decides to take over another, the aggressor may try to completely destroy its opponent with missile barrages or by sending in ground troops, thereby depriving the enemy of its warmaking ability. The data that defines the state could also be targeted for annihilation. This would include the national census, residential registration, and land registration information, tax and education data, and the laws and ordinances for governing the country. Buildings, roads, and bridges can be rebuilt if they are destroyed, but if all a state's essential data is erased or tampered with, it would be extremely difficult to restore.

If the data is lost, it is impossible to prove a person's existence or their identity, and the grounds for determining who owns what land will be gone. Land, individuals, and companies would also lose backing from the state, such as all the official documents attesting to their being. The state would meanwhile lose its ability to collect taxes from citizens and enterprises, thus rendering the national government incapable of functioning. The result would be a reset for the state and all its constituent elements, which would have nothing to show that they exist. Conceivably, an aggressor could rewrite the data and take everything away.

You might think that such critical data would never be deleted. However, the world has many countries that share borders and have hostile relations. It is entirely possible that an invading force could launch a surprise attack and seize the servers and data centers storing the data that defines the state. This is a problem not just for the state, but also smaller organizations such as local governments and companies. If corporate data for important technology falls into someone else's hands, the damage could be incalculable.

Data security is not just a concern relating to war and terrorism, but also disaster readiness. If a state or other organization loses its critical data, it becomes extremely difficult to recover and rebuild it. It must be protected against all eventualities, so that no matter what happens, it is not lost. This is why, just prior to Russia's invasion in February 2022, Ukraine hastily amended laws to encourage the use of cloud computing and safeguard the data defining its state at all costs.

Cybersecurity has always been a top priority for governments in this context, and great efforts have been made to protect systems from attacks. What is truly important, however, is not so much protecting systems as safeguarding the data within them.

If a state would collapse with the erasure of the data that defines it, then protecting that data may become a major focus of national security in the future. What kind of infrastructure would prevent data loss in times of war or disaster? What mechanisms can we build to prevent data from falling into the hands of invaders or terrorists? This is a perspective to keep in mind when considering data security.

Backups Aren't Enough

How can a state protect its data? The following sections will examine concrete methods for safeguarding data and how IOWN fits in.

Backups are the first conceivable line of defense. Multiple backups in different physical locations can further spread out risk. Those backups must occur more than just once a day or once a week. All of them have to happen in real time. Even if one day's worth of data is lost, that will take away the continuity of the organization's information, which can be severely difficult to recover.

Data movement to protect important information

When it comes to protecting data, however, backups are not enough. An organization also needs a way to move data at a moment's notice. Data movement capabilities address the risk that data could be stolen if a country's territory is invaded. If data is threatened, all of it must be transferred to a safe location instantly. Data is like a slippery fish that can easily escape your grasp. This kind of protection is essential for effective data defense.

At present, IOWN is the only technology capable of providing real-time backup and moving an enormous amount of data, such as that which defines a state. Real-time backup is a challenge over the internet, as transmission quality is not guaranteed and moving the data takes too much time. When protecting a state's data, it is important to build a network connecting multiple locations with a high-capacity, low-latency IOWN network that in the event of an emergency, can instantly move that data to a safe location. With such a system for safeguarding the data that defines a state, other countries cannot easily stage attacks against it.

What is a safe place to store data?

Where, then, is the safest place to store data? The answer is outer space. If, for example, all countries stored their crucial data in one location out in space, then no one would attack it. Furthermore, if humanity knew that we had to protect all our planet's data, world peace might come within our grasp.

Storing data in space might sound like an outlandish idea or something that could only happen in the far-off future. That, however, is not the case. As Chapter 4 explained, NTT launched NTT C89, a brand related to outer space, and is already moving ahead with a space data center business. We are also making steady progress with plans for computing in space, which involve linking satellites via optical communications to perform calculations as a distributed computer. Although there is insufficient transmission capacity and computing capability in space at this time, it is not such an implausible idea that in the future, we may store important data there.

Data holds the same importance for companies

So far, we have focused on the data belonging to a state, but the same circumstances also apply to corporate data. Whether it defines a state or a company, losing critical data would mean the end of that organization's existence.

To provide an example, NTT's crucial data would be our information on networks and our customers. If we were to lose all of this data, continuing our business would be impossible. We would be unable to properly operate our network equipment or receive payments from customers.

It turns out, even for us, safeguarding this essential data was once a blind spot. But as we gave deep thought to corporate sustainability, we realized the importance of securing the data that defines an organization. Therefore, we examined what data defines NTT, then listed up the top twenty types of data in this category. Next, we checked where this data was stored and how we were backing it up.

We were dumbfounded by the results. In some cases, backups were kept in very close proximity to the original data. The situation required an urgent response. It was disturbing to imagine what could have happened had there been a major disaster.

In the future, security measures will be about more than just dispersing backups of key data. It will also be important for companies to know where that data is and possess the ability to move it in an emergency. Industry's approach to data has thus far focused on how we can utilize it, but it is vital that we give data security the same degree of attention.

IOWN can safeguard organization-defining data

Taking this discussion of data security a step further, we come to the question: "What is my identity?" It is the data that distinguishes and defines us, is it not? If we do not safeguard the data that defines us, we may suffer the greatest loss of all, one that goes deeper than bodily or physical harm.

Here is an example to explain why. With accurate data on an individual's DNA, it may be possible to repair physical damage. Conversely, if preserving yourself is dependent upon having complete data about you, in the future, it may be possible to upload or move yourself online, far-fetched as this may sound.

Science-fiction novels, films, comic books, and animations have incorporated this idea into their plots. In one popular sci-fi TV show, the main character contracts an incurable disease and, on the verge of death, has their consciousness transplanted into an artificial life form. The information comprising the character's consciousness was separated from the body to live on in the information space. Episodes like this intersect with the idea of data defining the person.

More and more people today have an online avatar or other representation of themselves that they use to build communities. As the use of digital twins, which are virtual online spaces that resemble the real world, becomes more commonplace, the data that defines our online selves will become more and more synonymous with who we are. When we take that into consideration, a TV show episode where a person's consciousness lives on after the body dies does not seem so unrealistic.

If data defines a state, a company, or an individual, and it is that data by which it is sustained and endures, then we can consider the networks and computers which handle the data to be the lifelines making our world possible. From this perspective, building out the IOWN platform, which uses light, the fastest and most reliable form of data transmission, could hold significance for the entire world.

[Final Chapter]

From the Logic of Quantity
to the Logic of Values

From Quality to Quantity, from Quantity to Values

This book has thus far examined the concept behind IOWN, how far it has progressed, and what developments we can expect moving forward. In this final chapter, we will consider the relationship between IOWN and society. Let's delve into exactly how we are trying to reshape society with IOWN and toward what kind of future we are guiding it.

First, to clarify how IOWN will change society, we will review changes that have taken place in the business world over the past few decades.

Before the spread of the internet in the 1990s, the world was driven by the logic of quality. In that time, providing quality products and services created great value. Making good products led to a successful business. When the logic of quality reigned, Japan achieved great triumphs by pursuing a higher level of quality than other countries. The manufacturing industry in particular, including automobiles and electronic appliances, achieved impressively low prices and high quality through tireless quality improvement efforts, and the "Made in Japan" label soon became a symbol of quality across the globe. This also became the driving force behind Japan's rapid economic growth.

Japan lost out on the logic of quantity

The arrival of the internet was a game-changer for this dynamic. When the internet's proliferation ramped up in the mid-1990s, it rewrote the logic of quality and the world entered an era where the logic of quantity dominated.

The internet showed us that good quality is not always the top priority.

For example, if you open an online store, you can sell your products all over your country or even around the world. If your website can attract a lot of customers, you can lower your prices. Even if you have to compromise somewhat on quality, low-priced products will sell. And by bringing together a larger number of products, you can leverage them to create new business opportunities.

A prime example of this model is a new business that harnesses marketing data. The internet gives us a window into people's behavior. We can see who looked at what website, when, and what caught their interest. We can even see how they arrived at a purchasing decision. By collecting this data, we can gain a much clearer picture than ever before of what people want.

This mass collection of marketing data is a powerful weapon for developing and selling new products. Huge companies like GAFA in the United States have used the internet to collect tremendous amounts of data across borders. This has earned them enormous profits. The logic of quantity still rules the day.

Japan, however, has not been very adept at such accumulation of quantity. For example, when we rolled out the i-mode mobile internet service in Japan, we had aspirations of spreading it to other countries for users around the world. Unfortunately, despite being a huge hit in Japan, i-mode never caught on outside our country.

The cause seems to be that we failed to follow the business trend of winning by building quantity in the global market. When Apple later released its smartphone, the iPhone, it had a completely different result by transforming the mobile internet.

In other fields as well, many Japanese companies at the time were losing out in this world governed by the logic of quantity. Those that adapted and rose to the top were the companies that skillfully capitalized on the internet to amass quantity. In 1989, when Japan was at the height of its economic bubble, seven of the top ten companies in the world in terms of market capitalization were Japanese, but as of January 2024, not a single Japanese company is in the top twenty. The firms that took their place include tech companies that have grown rapidly under the internet's logic of quantity, such as Microsoft and Apple, which have often been the top two on the list.

Amassing quantity requires a global start

Why, then, has Japan failed to succeed in a world driven by the logic of quantity? Some say the size of the country's market is different. It is certainly true that the logic of quantity favors countries with large markets. A look around the world, however, reveals that there are countries that have worked hard and enjoyed success despite their small size.

Take, for example, Swedish company Ericsson. Sweden's population is just over 10 million, less than one-tenth that of Japan's, but Ericsson has the largest share of the market for 5G network infrastructure. The company has grown so important that the world's 5G networks would not exist without Ericsson. How did it manage to do that?

The answer lies in the different approaches taken by Japanese and Swedish companies. The former tend to first create and refine products in Japan, then release them to the world when they're fully developed. This is exactly the pattern we followed with i-mode.

However, Ericsson was developing products with the global market in mind from the very beginning. Rather than focusing on success in their own country, they first sought to build a global reputation. They would capture share in the global market, supply products to different countries, then finally bring those products back to their home country, where consumers could enjoy the benefits of lower prices. In contrast, many Japanese companies have never shaken off the assumption that if Japanese people like a product, it will surely sell well in the rest of the world. This may be the mistake we made in this era when the logic of quantity prevails.

In a sense, i-mode was a complete product. We carefully refined it in Japan before we embarked on a global launch. But when a product, service, or system becomes complete, it is very difficult to form partnerships and collaborate with other companies from that stage. As a result, you have to promote it on your own, and you end up competing with competitors who have teamed up against you. Amassing quantity is a challenge when attempted alone.

Lessons learned now applied to the IOWN Global Forum

We are applying the lessons we learned from i-mode to IOWN. The concept of IOWN covers an expansive range of domains, from telecommunications to semiconductors. It is by no means something NTT can create on its own, nor is it achievable without working with various companies and organizations. Therefore, our aim with IOWN was from the very beginning to build a global network of partners. It was important to get many companies and organizations, not just NTT, involved in the project from the outset and to have them bring their own technologies. To this end, we established the IOWN Global Forum in collaboration with Intel and Sony (now the Sony Group) and we recruited partners from around the world to help build IOWN.

Thanks to this approach, the number of companies and organizations involved has already greatly exceeded our initial expectations. At this stage, we can say we are making steady progress in building partnerships. Of course, those partners include companies that may be competitors farther down the road, but before we get to that point, they are important collaborators with whom we can engage in discussion and decision-making.

At the same time, we think it is important to provide the world with easy access to the photonics-electronics convergence technology that is central to IOWN. As explained in Chapter 2, NTT possesses the technology to miniaturize photonics-electronics convergence devices. That is why we established NTT Innovative Devices and have begun producing them. By supplying these devices to the world, the price of the entire system will decrease, facilitating its spread and yielding results that we can bring back to Japan.

Toward a logic of values fostering mutual respect

We have discussed how the internet shifted business from the logic of quality to the logic of quantity. But will the logic of quantity last forever? Probably not. People around the world hold various values which they each cherish. If we can learn to respect and appreciate these diverse values, then the next logical step will be a shift to the logic of values that emphasizes this mutual respect.

In a world that operates under the logic of values, adopting a global approach from the beginning holds even greater importance. That is because values throughout the world take on various forms. Some people in the world have thought processes and values that others may be unaware of or find incomprehensible. When we learn of these different values, we must deliver products and services that align with them accordingly.

At that moment, the question arises as to whether the infrastructure for a values-driven era should remain the internet. Has the time not come for a foundation that can deliver more diverse values worldwide without being bound by the framework of the internet, which is governed by the logic of quantity? With IOWN, we hope to develop infrastructure that supports an age of values across the planet.

For example, IOWN provides All-Photonics Network (APN) services. For each line that is installed, users can access various communications protocols, including TCP/IP, which is the communications protocol for the internet. This means that APNs can offer a much wider variety of services in addition to those available with the conventional internet. The IOWN network can provide such diverse services and values.

New social infrastructure requires a new philosophy

If networks and other key elements of social infrastructure undergo change, we will need a new philosophy. That is because as technology develops, we will face questions over how to approach and respond to the social issues that arise as a result.

Society and technology have a symbiotic relationship. While technology can change society, society can also impact technology, fostering and developing innovations. One recent example of technology changing society is the rapid evolution of generative AI. The greatest risk one senses from using it is a transformation of the space where discourse occurs. There is a possibility that it will destroy society's norms of right and wrong.

Consider, for example, social media posts. Individual posts may not have a huge influence, but if they are used to train generative AI, statements that were written with little concern about truthfulness could exert a powerful influence. It is also conceivable that generative AI could amplify misinformation and extreme arguments in such forums. This transformation of public discourse could exacerbate social divisions.

Or what about the digital twins that, as explained in Chapter 5, are virtual spaces that reproduce reality? If digital twins based on IOWN become commonplace, we may eventually be able to upload human consciousness in the form of data into a digital space. If people with money live on in these digital spaces while the rest of us simply perish along with our bodies, our world may end up being ruled by a select few, as suggested by Israeli historian Yuval Noah Harari in his book "Homo Deus: A Brief History of Tomorrow."

To prevent such scenarios and ensure that we do not lose sight of our direction as a society, we need a philosophy. New infrastructure requires a new philosophy.

Aiming for a society with multiple layers of values

NTT established the Kyoto Institute of Philosophy in July 2023 with Yasuo Deguchi, Dean and Professor of Philosophy at Kyoto University's Graduate School of Letters. Professor Deguchi and NTT Chairman Jun Sawada were appointed co-chairpersons. Society-altering technological innovations such as AI and IOWN are rapidly developing. As we integrate these technologies into society, how should our social infrastructure evolve and what global standards for values do we need in an era governed by the logic of values? Through its work and joint research, the institute is developing proposals to answer these questions. In other words, it is an attempt to construct new philosophical thought for a new era. With a diverse range of participants from industry, government, academia, and civil society from Japan and other countries, the Kyoto Institute of Philosophy aims to carry out work with international appeal from the historical and cultural city of Kyoto.

In the twentieth century, humanity made rapid advancements in science and technology while achieving economic prosperity. But did this really make us happier? There are certainly statistics around the world indicating improvements, such as much lower infant mortality and far fewer people suffering from extreme poverty. On the other hand, our world still has war and some people struggle to find happiness. Simply extending the status quo seems unlikely to bring about world peace or well-being.

"Moreover, as the world becomes more connected, it becomes increasingly evident that diverse values exist. It is clear now that when it comes to these values, there can be no single correct answer. We must now aspire to a society with multiple layers of values that coexist with each other. We must incorporate a new philosophy that allows the values of Western thought, which have been the de facto standard, and the values of Eastern thought, as well as the diverse values in different parts of the world, to coexist, as we use technology for good.

From the Digital to the Natural

Let's delve a little deeper into a society with multiple layers of values. What kind of technology does a society with diverse values need?

The natural world provides hints. German biologist Jakob von Uexküll proposed the concept of Umwelt, which states that all living things possess their own unique perceptions and live within their own worlds.

For example, although ultraviolet rays are invisible to the human eye, birds and insects can see them. In other words, the world or Umwelt that we humans experience is completely different from that of other creatures. Using bees as an example, a flower is merely pretty to the human eye, but in a bee's vision, it has a center with nectar that is highlighted by ultraviolet light. This is the Umwelt of a bee. However, we have built today's digital world using only what we need from the broader, more diverse information out in nature. That is why, for example, the Umwelt of bees is completely absent from our current digital world.

Just as with one's Umwelt, what a person in human society values will differ depending on the individual and their culture. Given that, if we can meticulously obtain and layer data that has not been valued in the past, we may be able to accommodate various values in multiple layers. By retrieving information that has been overlooked in the digital world, we can bring it closer to the natural world. Such technology and approaches may be what a society with multiple layers of values requires.

Our world also contains a wealth of information that is beyond the grasp of human senses. By obtaining such information with sensors and utilizing it, we should be able to address issues in society and open up a new world.

Consider today's rapidly evolving generative AIs. To put it simply, they are trained on correlations between words so they can produce sentences with meaning. If we take this a step further, we could eventually train them on correlations between not just words, but also data such as images and quantities. This may allow us to solve previously intractable problems.

Why does the SARS-CoV-2 virus that causes COVID-19 mutate? Analyzing human language will not arrive at an answer. However, training an AI with data on earlier viruses could provide clues. Likewise, solutions to many problems may exist in living organisms, nature, the Earth, or in outer space, but finding them requires the collection of a vast amount of data.

The world is fascinated with generative AI at the moment, but at this point, it is still simply searching for answers to truths and realities that exist only in the human world. To find answers in the next era, however, we must expand our data collection beyond our species' world to encompass the Earth and space. Otherwise, we will not solve the problems in the natural world such as pandemics and climate change.

If we are to attempt this, we would have to handle an exponentially larger quantity of data. The enormous energy consumption for computations by generative AI employing human language is already a serious issue right now. If we were to try to expand this technology's scope to the planet or space, we would have nowhere near enough energy.

The way to find a solution is, of course, light. If we do not transition from electricity to light and dramatically increase energy efficiency, we will sooner or later reach a limit. In the future, IOWN will be the foundation for us to advance innovation beyond human limits.

What Is the Identity of IOWN?

This book has introduced IOWN from various angles, including how it works, the framework for its development, and use cases in the near future.

In technical terms, IOWN uses light to replace the electricity currently used in communications and computing. Light has a much higher transmission capacity than electricity and is far more energy efficient. By gradually miniaturizing the devices that convert electricity to light and expanding the use of light from network equipment to computers and then to chips, we can reduce energy consumption while significantly improving the performance of communications and computing.

When we examine the impact that IOWN will have on society, it becomes evident that this technological platform holds great potential. It will serve as a foundation that contributes to progress toward solutions for a number of issues in society, such as climate change and aging populations with declining birthrates, while also taking a nature-positive approach that halts and then reverses the loss of biodiversity. Furthermore, it will contribute to greater respect for diverse values, human happiness, and better lives.

What is the identity of IOWN? From a technical perspective, it is a barrier-breaking innovation that significantly pushes out the limits of existing technology. And from a social perspective, we believe it is a light of hope for the future that will restore Earth to a sustainable planet where people and nature coexist.

What kind of future will we create with IOWN? That depends on all of us living now and into the future.

Afterword

The idea behind IOWN, of using light to replace the electricity that has powered our networks and computing thus far, was first conceived in the 1960s, when NTT began researching optical communications. However, it was difficult to miniaturize the photonics-electronics convergence devices required to convert between electricity and light. Reducing power consumption was also quite difficult.

In 2019, however, we finally made a breakthrough. Using a structure called a photonic crystal, which we had spent many years researching, we created the world's first optical modulator, a device that generates optical signals, and optical transistor operating with extremely low power consumption.

This innovation in photonics-electronics convergence technology enabled IOWN APN (All-Photonics Network) services that use only light and paved the way toward light-based computing. A future that had been beyond the limits of human technology suddenly appeared before us.

Whenever I explain what IOWN is, I like to describe it as "unlimited innovation." This does not simply mean shattering the limitations of individual technologies such as computational and transmission speeds. With IOWN, we can paint a picture of a new future by leaping past the limits of our thinking that is premised on the technologies at our disposal now, such as the assumption that we should charge our smartphones daily or that networks will inevitably experience latency. This is what I have in mind when I describe IOWN as unlimited innovation.

Our society faces many challenges. Some, such as climate change, are so vexing it is tempting to throw one's hands in the air and give up on finding a solution. However, there are times in history when humanity has made unexpected breakthroughs thanks to innovative ideas and technology that enable great strides toward solutions. We consider the development of photonics-electronics convergence technology in 2019 to be one such breakthrough.

For the Key People section in Chapter 3, President Rong-Shy Lin of Chunghwa Telecom in Taiwan and Vice President of Wireline Networks & Infrastructure Gilles Bourdon of Orange Innovation in France agreed to be featured, as they understand and endorse the contents of this book. I would like to express my heartfelt gratitude to both for taking the time out of their busy schedules to assist us. I would also like to express my sincere appreciation to I would also like to express my sincere appreciation to Naohiko Morimoto, the Prime Account Director and General Manager at AKKODiS Consulting's IOWN Promotion Office, for his invaluable support in providing the case studies for Chapter 1.

This book was created to present NTT's strong desire to contribute to global sustainability through IOWN, and with the hope of winning understanding and endorsement from as large an audience as possible about the IOWN Initiative by introducing what this technology platform is and the sort of world we are seeking to make possible with it.

The realization of innovative photonics-electronics convergence technology enabled the IOWN Initiative's birth. It is still in its infancy, and in order to grow big and strong, it needs many friends. Nothing would make me happier as an author than for this book to serve as a catalyst for people to learn about IOWN and consider how we can use this technology to create a better society.

Katsuhiko Kawazoe
Senior Executive Vice President, CTO of NTT

161

Reference List

Chapter 3

1. "Latest Activities in the IOWN Global Forum", NTT Technical Review, February 2024: https://doi.org/10.53829/ntr202402fa1

Chapter 4

1. "Move Aside, Crypto. AI Could Be The Next Climate Disaster.", Gizmodo, April 3, 2023: https://gizmodo.com/chatgpt-ai-openai-carbon-emissions-stanford-report-1850288635

2. "AI Research Rankings 2022: Sputnik Moment for China?", Medium, May 20, 2022: https://thundermark.medium.com/ai-research-rankings-2022-sputnik-moment-for-china-64b693386a4

3. "More Agents Is All You Need", arXiv, February 3, 2024: https://arxiv.org/html/2402.05120v1

4. "Extracting Concepts from GPT-4", OpenAI, June 6, 2024: https://openai.com/index/extracting-concepts-from-gpt-4/

5. "NTT and Sakana AI sign a collaboration agreement for the R&D of AI constellations that will enable a society in which sustainable generative AI is used.", NTT, Sakana AI, November 13, 2023: https://group.ntt/en/newsrelease/2023/11/13/231113b.html

6. "Improvement of working environment and safety of construction work by remote operation of construction equipment and monitoring of site environment by IOWN APN", NTT, November 9, 2023: https://group.ntt/en/newsrelease/2023/11/09/231109b.html

7. "IOWN APN begins demonstration of robot operation and sharing of the same environment to support remote surgery: Achieving an environment that makes sites over 100 km apart resemble the same operating room", NTT, Medicaroid, November 15, 2022: https://group.ntt/en/newsrelease/2022/11/15/221115a.html

8. "NTT and Olympus Begin World's First Joint Demonstration Experiment of Cloud Endoscopy System: Cloud endoscopy system using NTT's high-speed, low-latency IOWN APN technology", NTT, Olympus, March 27, 2024: https://group.ntt/en/newsrelease/2024/03/27/240327b.html

9. "'Meiji Yasuda J League World Challenge 2023 powered by docomo' ni oite APN IOWN1.0 wo Katsuyou shi Realtime-sei ga Motomerareru 'Remote Production' to '8KVR Fukusuu Douji Eizou Densou' no Jisshou wo Jisshi" [Demonstration at the Meiji Yasuda J.League World Challenge 2023 Powered by Docomo: Utilized APN IOWN 1.0 to Conduct Remote Production and 8K VR with Multiple Simultaneous Video Transmission Requiring Real-Time Performance], Japan Professional Football League, NTT, July 24, 2023: https://group.ntt/jp/newsrelease/2023/07/24/230724b.html (Japanese)

10. "Kizon WAN Service to no Seinou Hikaku" [Performance Comparison with Existing WAN Service], NTT East: https://business.ntt-east.co.jp/content/iown/comparison/ (Japanese)

11. "Nihonhatsu! APN IOWN1.0 wo Katsuyou Shita esports Event no Jitsuen 'Open New Gate for esports 2023 ~ IOWN ga Tsukuru esports no Mirai ~'" [First Esports Event in Japan Utilizing APN IOWN 1.0: Open New Gate for Esports 2023 – The Future of Esports Created by IOWN], NTT e-Sports, March 2, 2023: https://www.ntte-sports.co.jp/media/2023/03/02/106 (Japanese)

12. "Sekaihatsu, Toukyuu Fudousan to NTT Group Kouiki Shibuyaken Machizukuri he no IOWN Senkou Dounyuu ~ 'Shoku - Jyuu - Yuu' wo Yuugou Shita Kankyou Senshin Toshi no Gugenka ~" [In World's First, Tokyu Land Corporation and NTT Group Introduce IOWN for Urban Development in Greater Shibuya: Embodiment of an Environmentally Advanced City Fusing Work, Living, and Leisure], Tokyu Land Corporation, NTT, NTT Docomo, June 6, 2023: https://group.ntt/jp/newsrelease/2023/06/07/230607a.html (Japanese)

13. "Business Strategy in the Field of Space Business", NTT, June 3, 2024: https://group.ntt/en/newsrelease/2024/06/03/240603a.html

Writing Contributors

Shingo Kinoshita
Senior Vice President, Head of Research and Development Planning Department,
Research and Development Market Strategy Division, NTT

Yosuke Aragane
Vice President, Head of IOWN Development Office, Research and Development
Planning Department, Research and Development Market Strategy Division, NTT

Hidehiro Tsukano
President and CEO, NTT Innovative Devices

Masahito Tomizawa
Senior Executive Vice President and CTO, NTT Innovative Devices

Production Contributors

Takanori Watanabe
Tomomi Kouyama
Public Relations Department, NTT

The Identity of IOWN
Unlimited Innovation by NTT

First edition published: April 14, 2025

Authors: Akira Shimada, Katsuhiko Kawazoe
Issuer: Takeshi Matsui
Publisher: Nikkei Business Publications, Inc.
Seller: Nikkei BP Marketing, Inc.
4-3-12 Toranomon, Minato-ku, Tokyo 105-8308
Book designers: Shohei Oguchi and Tsumugi Kanda (tobufune)
Production and DTP: Naoya Matsukawa (Nikkei BP Consulting, Inc.)
Editor: Hironori Watanabe
Editing assistant: Toru Izumoi
Cover photographer: Junya Inagaki
Translator: Alexander Farrell
Translation editor: Hirohisa Tanizaki
Translation agency: Archi-Voice Co., Ltd.
Printer and binder: Dai Nippon Printing Co., Ltd.

Unauthorized duplication or reproduction (including photocopying) of this book is prohibited, unless otherwise permitted under copyright law. Digitalization and conversion to an electronic format by a third party other than the purchaser is not permitted, including for personal use. Use the below contact information for inquiries or correspondence concerning this book.
https://nkbp.jp/booksQA

The Identity of IOWN
Unlimited Innovation by NTT

2025年4月14日　第1版第1刷発行

著者　島田明　川添雄彦
発行者　松井健
発行　株式会社日経BP
発売　株式会社日経BPマーケティング
〒105-8308 東京都港区虎ノ門4-3-12
ブックデザイン　小口翔平＋後藤司（tobufune）
制作・DTP　松川直也（株式会社日経BPコンサルティング）
編集　渡辺博則
編集協力　出雲井亨
カバー写真　稲垣純也
翻訳　株式会社アーキ・ヴォイス
翻訳者　アレクサンダー・ファレル
翻訳編集者　谷崎弘尚
印刷・製本　大日本印刷株式会社

本書の無断複写・複製（コピーなど）は著作権法上の例外を除き、禁じられています。購入者以外の第三者による電子データ化および電子書籍化は、私的使用を含め一切認められておりません。
本書籍に関するお問い合わせ、ご連絡は下記にて承ります。
https://nkbp.jp/booksQA

ISBN 978-4-296-20762-6
Printed in Japan
©Nippon Telegraph and Telephone Corporation 2025